# The LIFE Plan

*Volume Five*
*The Church*

By Allen L. Elder

ISBN: 978-1-6923-4271-5

# DEDICATION

The LIFE Plan in its entirety is dedicated to the members of Bethany Baptist Church of Spartanburg, South Carolina where the material was written and used for the very first time.

## Table of Contents

# INTRODUCTION

When I was six years old, I was born again into the family of God and became a follower of the Lord Jesus Christ. Almost immediately, I knew that I wanted to be in the ministry. For the next several years, I attended church and learned many facts about God and the Bible. However, I did not learn what to do with all of that information. No one intentionally and strategically discipled me into the purpose of God for my life. Frustrated by years of learning with no practical guidance, I walked away from the church. Another ten years went by before God put a leader in front of me who invited me to follow him as he followed Christ.

After twenty years of being a Christian, I was of not much use to the cause of Christ. After high school and the USAF, I started going to church with my girlfriend who later became my wife. It was then that God put some key people before me who taught me and led me with purpose. It made all the difference and I began to get some real traction in my life. Now, more than thirty years of ministry later, I can share The LIFE Plan with you to help you on your journey.

The LIFE Plan is a discipleship curriculum which takes you from a beginning with God into a life lived according to his purpose and for his glory. From it you will gain a grasp on the story and structure of the Bible, and on the Bible's strategy of spiritual reproduction and multiplication. You will also learn how to discover God's purpose for your own life so that you can serve him in the way he has designed you to serve.

The LIFE Plan is made up of six volumes containing 216 total lessons. Each lesson has a short text followed by a lesson outline, Scripture references, pathways for deeper study, and with questions which underscore the important truths from the lessons that you will need to know and understand. Some questions ask for your personal response which will help you to apply the material in your own life. The lessons are structured in the following way.

Volume One - The Bible's Story (Genesis 1-11)
Volume Two - The Bible's Story (Genesis 12- Malachi)
Volume Three - The Structure of the Entire Bible
Volume Four - The Life of Christ on Earth
Volume Five - The Church
Volume Six - Your Personal Ministry

With The LIFE Plan, you will be equipped with a knowledge of the Bible that will help you find your way through life. With the materials in hand, you will also be equipped to guide another person and other people to find their way as well. In so doing, you will be investing your life into others in fulfilment of the Lord's great commission to make disciples of all nations. Living your life intentionally in this way will indeed prepare you for eternity where you will give an accounting of what you did with that which God gave you on earth. If you are as I am, when the day comes when I stand before God, I will want to have lived my life on earth with eternity in mind.

The LIFE Plan is intended to be a curriculum from which you can learn and with which you can teach another disciple. There is no limit to what can be done with these lessons. They can be used in a variety of ways and for a variety of ministries. Following are some suggested ways to use the material.

1. Children's Ministry
2. Youth Ministry
3. Sunday School
4. Small Groups
5. Prison Ministry
6. Personal Discipling
7. Correspondence Course
8. In School and After School Programs
9. Sports Ministries
10. Missions
11. Bible Schools
12. Personal Study
13. Family Devotions
14. Online Studies

Our hope is that you will use these studies to reproduce reproducing disciples of Christ around the world. And we would love to hear about how you will use them. May God bless you as you learn and grow and invest into the lives of others.

Allen L. Elder

# 1. CHRIST IS THE HEAD OF THE CHURCH

## THEME: CHRIST: THE HEAD OF THE BODY

BLOCK 5 - THEME 1 - LESSON 1

**LESSON AIM:** The lesson shows the prominent place Jesus holds in the church.

**SCRIPTURE:** (Ephesians 1:19-23)

Our lessons this year will be all about the church. When we think of church, we may think of a traditional brick building with a steeple and stained glass windows where people go to worship. Or, we may think of a store-front building where churches pop up more and more today. Whatever picture comes to our minds when we think of the church, this is only a part of the whole concept of church. We are going to learn more about the church this year, including what it is, what it does, who it is made of, and why it should be a very important part of our lives.

Our first lesson speaks of Jesus Christ as the head of the church. We will learn that the church is the body of Christ in the world. And every living body needs a head, doesn't it? Well, the church, the body of Christ, needs a head also, and this head is Jesus Christ. Let's try to understand what this means.

On one occasion when Jesus was talking with his disciples, he said that the church belonged to him. He said to them, "I will build *my* church." (Matthew 16:18). This is the first thing we need to understand about the church; the church belongs to God. The church is not something that belongs to us. In this sense, we do not have the final say on the things we should do as a church. God has already told us in the Bible what he wants the church to be and do. The thing we need to do is to read and study the Bible to learn what God has told us about the church and about its mission in the world. Then, we need to do what the Bible tells us to do. Since the church belongs to God, he has the final say on what he wants the church to do in the world.

Since the church belongs to God, God has made Jesus the head of the church. Let's consider three facts about Christ as head of the church. To be head of the church is a place of position. Speaking of these things to the Ephesians, Paul mentions several things about this position. It is a position of resurrection. Through his power, God raised Christ from the dead. Christ's position is also in a seat at God's right hand. This is a place of honor, power, and authority, and is his position as head of the church. All these things are part of what Paul wrote to the Philippians about how God had exalted Jesus after he was obedient unto death on the cross (Philippians 2:5-11). God has given Jesus an exalted position over all creation. This is recognized best as it relates to his position as head of the church.

Christ's position as head of the church is also a place of power. Paul gave us five categories of opposition to Christ in which his power is greater. His power is greater than that of principalities, or rulers. Throughout history, many men have been called the most powerful man on earth. God is greater and more powerful than all of them. Read Daniel 4 in the Old Testament about the personal account of how King Nebuchadnezzar of ancient Babylon learned this lesson the hard way. The President of the United States of America is often called the most powerful man in the free world. His power is no match for the power of God. The Bible says, "*The king's heart is in the hand of the LORD, as the rivers of water: he turneth it whithersoever he will. (Proverbs 21:1) KJV.*

Christ's position as head of the church is more powerful than other powers, or jurisdictions, of world rules. In fact, Christ has all authority in heaven and on earth (Matthew 28:18). He is more powerful than any other might, or force, that may be rallied on earth. He is more powerful than any dominion, or government, in the history of the world. And his position of power is more than that of any name, or individual personality, you can think of. In short, there is no one or no thing that is more powerful than the exalted, seated, ruling, reigning Lord Jesus Christ. It is this all-powerful (omnipotent) God who is the head of the church. No wonder Jesus said that the gates of hell could not prevail against his church (Matthew 16:18).

Finally, Christ's position as head of the church is the place of practical function for the church. Christ's function can be seen in the things he does on behalf of the church. He is the church's redeemer; he gave himself as a ransom for his people. He is the head which speaks of guidance and protection. And he is the chief leader of the church, or the chief shepherd.

We can also see his position as head in the things he does for the church. Think of all the things your physical body does through its head. A body thinks, sees, speaks, listens, eats, and breathes through its head. How much better off do you think the body of Christ would be if it did those things through its head (Christ), too? This is exactly what Christ wants to be for the church. The functions of Christ for the church have been given to us in the Bible. A church that wants to be pleasing to Christ only has to find his instructions in the Bible and follow them. Let us be this kind of body for Christ. Let us be a body that completes the commands it is given through its head so that Christ may be honored and that the mission of the church in the world can be accomplished.

As a Christian, you are a part of the body of Christ. Take some time to properly align yourself with the head of the body. Recognize and admit that Christ is the head and that we are just a part of the body. Every part of the body is subject to the head. No part of the body is greater than the head. Whatever role God has given you in his body, give yourself to him that you might fulfill this role in just the way he envisioned that you would fulfill it when he placed you in this role. Doing so will bring much satisfaction into your life as you learn to complete the assignment that God has given to you as a part of his body, the church.

**CHRIST IS THE HEAD OF THE CHURCH**
**BLOCK 5 - THEME 1 - LESSON 1 (145 OF 216)**
**LESSON OUTLINE**

To be the head of the church is:

**I A PLACE OF POSITION**
- A. Raised from the dead.
- B. Seated at God's right hand.

**II A PLACE OF POWER**

Oppositions to Christ's power:
- A. Principalities
- B. Powers
- C. Might
- D. Dominion
- E. Name

**III A PLACE OF PRACTICAL FUNCTION**
- A. What Christ does on behalf of the church
  1. Redeem.
  2. Head
     a. Guide
     b. Protect
  3. Chief leader

- B. What Christ, as head, does for the church
  1. Thinks
  2. Sees
  3. Speaks
  4. Listens
  5. Eats
  6. Breathes

**SCRIPTURES TO BROADEN YOUR UNDERSTANDING**

1. The body of Christ
   1 Corinthians 12
   Ephesians 2:11-22
   Ephesians 5:21-33

2. Christ as head of the body
   Ephesians 1:20-23
   Colossians 1:18

3. The church's mission
   Matthew 28:18-20
   Acts 1:8

4. Christ's humility and exaltation
   Philippians 2:5-11

**LINES OF THEOLOGICAL CONNECTION**

1. CHRISTOLOGY
   Christ's authority
   Judgement given to Christ
   Christ as redeemer
   Christ as the chief shepherd

2. GOD'S ATTRIBUTES
   Omnipotence

3. ECCLESIOLOGY
   The church is Christ's body
   The church is subject to Christ

**LESSON GLOSSARY**

1. Omnipotent
   All powerful.

2. Emplaced
   To be positioned

**CHRIST IS THE HEAD OF THE CHURCH**
**BLOCK 5 - THEME 1 - LESSON 1 (145 OF 216)**
**QUESTIONS**

1. How do we learn what God has told us about the church and its mission in the world?

2. What illustration does the Bible use for the church?

3. In what ways is the church like a body?

4. What part of the body is Jesus?

5. To whom does the church belong?

6. Who has the final say on what he wants the church to do in the world?

7. What are some of the functions Christ does on behalf of the church?

8. List five things in the world that stand in opposition to Christ as head of the church.

9. What part of the body of Christ do you think you are?

# 2. GROW UP INTO CHRIST

## THEME: CHRIST: THE HEAD OF THE BODY

BLOCK 5 - THEME 1 - LESSON 2

**LESSON AIM:** Show that our relationship with Christ should result in growth and spiritual health in ourselves and in the body of Christ.

**SCRIPTURE:** (Ephesians 4:11-16)

As head of the body, Christ has done many wonderful things for his church. Another one of those things is mentioned in this passage. He has given gifts to the church. These gifts are the people he has given us to encourage, prepare, and help us along in our spiritual growth. As a believer, we have to remember and often remind ourselves that we are a part of a body. We are not a lone wolf who is free to go off in his own direction. The things we do now as Christians must be done for the good of the body.

Christ has given us teaching-pastors (v11-12) to prepare us to occupy the place in the body of Christ here God has designed for us to serve. Concerning our place in the body of Christ, we can learn several more things from verse 12. Since God has given us a place in the body, it is in the church where we find belonging. One of the things people long for and desperately need to know is that they are important and that they are needed. In no other place or role on earth can one find belonging on the scale of what it means to belong to the body of Christ. This belonging then, fosters self-esteem and reminds us that our life is significant.

Since God has given us a place in the body, this means that we have a particular function in that place. Think of the parts which make up your physical body. Every part is in the place where it belongs and it has a job to do there. What would happen if you had a forearm growing out of your forehead? You would realize that something was wrong, wouldn't you? You would realize that your forearm could not fulfill its intended role as long as it was out of its place in your body. And, you would also know that your forearm was hindering the work of the forehead by being out of place. It is vital that we discover the place and part in the body where God had given us to live and work.

It is also important that we know that in the place where God has designed for us to serve, we have to grow and be a healthy part of the body. If we are unhealthy or underdeveloped, the body cannot function to its full capacity. Have you ever had to limp on a sore ankle? You cannot stand, walk, or run in a normal way. Other muscles are called on by the body to get you where you need to go. When we are not growing and are not spiritually healthy as Christians, we are a hindrance to the body of Christ.

The last thing we see in verse 12 is that we exist for the good of the body. Take away any part of your body and it cannot live by itself. It is by remaining in the body, being healthy, and fulfilling its intended role that the parts of the body contribute to the overall health and service of the body. As Christians, we must learn to be more attentive to the decisions we make in our lives and how they will affect the church, the body of Christ. Everything we do should be done for the good of the body.

Verse 13 comes at a good place in the passage because it tells us how we can check ourselves to see if we are in the right place in the body and if we are functioning properly in that place. To do this, we are to measure ourselves by the standard of Jesus Christ himself. Other people can be an encouragement to us and we may be inspired to serve in a better way as we watch how other people serve. But we cannot measure ourselves totally by the standard of other people for the following reasons. First, and obviously, the Bible tells us to measure ourselves by the standard of Christ. Any other standard is an improper measurement. And, people are also in the process of measuring themselves by Christ, therefore they are an incomplete standard of measurement. Finally, that which you use to measure yourself is what you will become. Measure yourself by Christ and you will become more like Jesus.

Growing up into Christ also means that we must be established in the body of doctrine and belief that the Bible presents. The Bible gives us the mind, will, and heart of God. It tells us what God wants and expects from us as his people. In most cases, this is simple and straightforward. But, we have to remember that we have an adversary who is trying to draw us away from God and obedience to him. He specializes in taking the simple, straightforward statements of God and twists them to say something other than what God has said. Remember his first words to Eve in the Garden of Eden, "Yea, hath God said...?" We have to read and study God's Word so we can know what God has said and what he wants, but also so we can recognize when something false is presented to us as if it were the Word of God.

It is important for us to believe right so we can behave right. When we are not sure what to believe, or what we believe, we can be pushed and tossed about like a small sailboat on a stormy ocean. Belief anchors us on the stormy seas of life so that we can be calm, steady, and sure of Christ when things happen to try to shake our trust in him. You must read the Bible for yourself and depend on the Holy Spirit to help you understand it, believe it, and apply it to your life. This will prevent you from being deceived when non-truths come your way.

In verses 15 and 16, we can see the importance of all of this. The good of the body is at stake. Every part of the body is important. Every part has a job to do. And every part is connected to some other parts of the body. These other parts receive part of their health and nourishment through our parts. It is only when we are all in the correct place and functioning properly that the whole body can truly be whole. Every one of us is a contributor to the wholeness and wellness of the body. When we are in our places and fulfilling our roles, the body can grow, be healthy, and work as God wants it to work for his purpose in the world.

If you are a Christian, you are a part of Christ's body, the church. He has a specific place where he wants you to be and a specific work he wants you to do. In order to fulfill this place, you must grow up unto Christ. You must do as Paul said in another place, "Take the time and the trouble to keep yourself spiritually fit. Grow in Christ. Fulfill your place in the body. Be a contributor to its health and service.

**GROW UP INTO CHRIST**
**BLOCK 5 - THEME 1 - LESSON 2 (146 OF 216)**
**LESSON OUTLINE**

**I GROW INTO YOUR PLACE IN THE BODY OF CHRIST**
A. Find belonging
B. Find a function (have a purpose)
C. Be healthy
D. Exist for the good of the whole body

**II MEASURE YOUR GROWTH BY THE STANDARD OF CHRIST**
A. Belief
B. Behavior

**SCRIPTURES TO BROADEN YOUR UNDERSTANDING**

1. Doctrine
   Romans 15:4
   2 Timothy 3:10-17

2. Growing in Christ
   Mark 3:14
   2 Timothy 2:15
   1 Peter 2:2
   2 Peter 3:18

**LINES OF THEOLOGICAL CONNECTION**

1. ECCLESIOLOGY
   The church as a body
   Spiritual gifts
   Ministerial roles
2. THEOLOGY
   Biblical Theology
   Systematic Theology
   Historical Theology
   Dogmatic Theology
   Contemporary Theology

**LESSON GLOSSARY**

1. Doctrine
   A body of belief or teaching.

**GROW UP INTO CHRIST**
**BLOCK 5 - THEME 1 - LESSON 2 (146 OF 216)**
**QUESTIONS**

1. Name one thing from this lesson of which a Christian must remind himself.

2. What is a great benefit of being a member of the body of Christ?

3. What is the purpose of having people in specific positions in the body?

4. Why is it important that a Christian find his place in the body of Christ?

5. What one thing should we consider in all of our decisions?

6. By whose standard are we to measure ourself?

7. Why is it important to measure yourself by the standard of Christ?

8. Why does reading the Bible anchor us when our faith is shaken?

# 3. THE PREEMINENCE OF CHRIST

## THEME: CHRIST: THE HEAD OF THE BODY

BLOCK 5 - THEME 1 - LESSON 3

**LESSON AIM:** Show that Christ has first place in the church.

**SCRIPTURE:** (Colossians 1:18)

The time in which we live is characterized by many churches which are struggling to keep their doors open and their ministries functioning. In the Southern Baptist Convention of which we are a part, around eighty percent of the churches are in this situation. Many of them do not know what to do to correct their problem. It is predicted that if some change is not made soon, within the next five years, twenty-five percent of our total church force (SBC) will close their doors and go out of business. This would total some 11,500 churches.

Local churches struggle for many reasons. Sometimes the pastor may not be able to lead the church as he should. Sometimes there can be a power struggle within the leadership of the church between the pastor and the deacons which results in an unhealthy church. And sometimes, the problem can be with the congregation. They simply refuse to be led and refuse to go in the ways of the Lord. There are many varieties of problems among each of these three scenarios mentioned above.

In the lives of individual Christians, the same indifference, apathy, and rebellion can be seen. People often try to live their lives without regard for the ways of the Lord. They try to live life on their own terms. They travel to the beat of a different drum, as it has been said. And, like the churches of today, many people find themselves in a similar situation on a personal level. They look at themselves and their life is a mess. Everything seems to be wrong and hardly anything ever seems to go in their favor. There are difficult obstacles in their way in each direction they turn. The home life is suffering. The family is at odds against each other. The job is not working out. Their life seems like one long struggle day after day after day.

In each example above, the problems are similar and the reason for them is typically the same: either the church or the person does not recognize Jesus Christ in the rightful place where he belongs. In the church and in the individual life, Jesus should be preeminent.

There is a similar word to the word "preeminence" which we often substitute in our church and in our life. It is the word "prominence". It sounds close to the same but has a much different meaning. To be prominent is to be recognized as important but not necessarily exclusive. To be preeminent is to be in first place in all things. For many churches, and for many people, Jesus is prominent, but he is not preeminent.

They know that he should be important, but they would rather exert their own will above his, robbing him of the preeminence he should have. This is the reason for the condition of many dead and dying churches, and for the never-ending struggle in the lives of many people. They are swimming against the current, so to speak. As long as this condition continues, the outcome will remain the same.

What does it mean when we talk about the preeminence of Christ? First it means that we must recognize and acknowledge the place Jesus holds in all things. Jesus should be first, plainly and simply. When God began to reveal his ways unto man in the form of laws and commands, his first command to man was that he would have no other gods before him. This carries over into our relationship with Christ and the church. Christ should be first in all things.

Referring to himself when speaking to John, Jesus said, "I am Alpha and Omega, the beginning and the end, the first and the last." This statement does at least two things. It is a statement about the Deity of Christ, first of all. By saying he is the first and the last, he is repeating the same phrase used by Jehovah in the Old Testament about himself. Jesus is saying that he and the Father are one and the same God. Second, he is saying that as God, there should be no other thing or person in our lives to occupy this position, or place.

In reference to the church, the preeminence of Christ is recognized in his position as head of the body. Jesus is the firstborn from the dead. The resurrection of Christ from the dead was a picture of what happens to every person who believes on Jesus as the Messiah. Within their spirit, they are raised from the spiritual death that sin caused in man in the Garden of Eden. The church is made of those whom God has brought back from spiritual death, and Jesus is the first in line among those who make up the church. He is head of the body, or head of the church.

To say that Christ is preeminent also is a recognition and acknowledgement of Christ's purpose for the church. Christ is on a rescue mission. He is in the process of rescuing men, women, boys, and girls from among all peoples of the earth who are still among those who are spiritually dead. Jesus came to the earth and died on a cross to bring the means of salvation that would bring God and man together again. He commissioned his followers to go to all peoples of the earth with this message of the good news of salvation through him. To fulfill this purpose of God is the one and only all-inclusive reason for a church to exist. When a church makes the Great Commission their first and only priority, they will be able to continue their mission into the world. When they discount or completely disobey this purpose of God for the church, they fall into the problems we mentioned in the beginning of this study.

The same holds true in the lives of individual Christians. We are a part of the church. And, God's purpose for the church is also his purpose for each one of us on an individual basis. He intends to send us on a mission with him for the rescue of the spiritually lost. Regardless of what occupation we may have or where in the world life may take us, we are to be about this mission with God. When we choose to disregard this mission, we encounter the disintegration of our lives that occurs when the purpose of God is not the first priority of our life.

Let's clarify one issue brought up by what we have said about the preeminence of Christ. We are not saying that when Jesus is in first place in your life or in your church, or that when his purpose is your first and only priority, that you will not encounter any more difficult situations. To live for God does not mean that life goes on smoothly and never is hard or difficult. The truth is, if and when we surrender to Jesus' rightful place and purpose in our life and church, things might even become harder. We are not given immunity from difficulty just because we are following

Jesus. There is the testimony of many a life that would show that to follow God completely did mean great difficulty, maybe even to the point of physical death. But, when we surrender to the preeminence of Jesus recognized in his place and purpose, we are putting ourselves into a position of obedience to God, and in a position of realizing his promise to be with us, even to the ends of the earth until the end of time, come what may. The road before us may be steep and difficult, but it will lead us to the kind of impact in the world for Christ that God so desires for us to have.

As you think about your own life, what place does Jesus occupy in your life? Is it no place at all? Is it a place of prominence? Or, is it a place of preeminence? What about the things for which you are giving your life? Are you living for yourself and your own selfish ambitions and fleshly desires? Or, do you want to live according to God's purpose and be a part of the global harvest of souls from among all the peoples of the earth? Your answers to these questions will determine whether you merely spend and waste the life God has given you on earth, or whether you invest it and reproduce it into his global cause. The only wise thing to do, in the light of eternity, is to surrender to the preeminence of Christ. Acknowledge him as the occupant of first place and first purpose in your life and in your church.

**THE PREEMINENCE OF CHRIST**
**BLOCK 5 - THEME 1 - LESSON 3 (147 OF 216)**
**LESSON OUTLINE**

Prominence vs. preeminence

The preeminence of Christ expresses:

**I THE PLACE JESUS HOLDS**
A. In the church
B. In our lives

**II THE PURPOSE JESUS HAS**
A. For the church
B. For the individual

**SCRIPTURES TO BROADEN YOUR UNDERSTANDING**

1. Jesus as first
   Revelation 1:11

2. No other gods
   Exodus 20:3

3. Christ as firstborn from the dead
   1 Corinthians 15:20

4. Christ as head
   Ephesians 1:20-23
   Colossians 1:12-20

5. Jesus came to save sinners
   1 Timothy 1:15

**LINES OF THEOLOGICAL CONNECTION**

1. CHRISTOLOGY
   The preeminence of Christ
   Christ as head of the church
   Christ's purpose in the world

2. ECCLESIOLOGY
   Christians are subject unto Christ
   The Great Commission

**LESSON GLOSSARY**

1. Prominence
   A place of importance

2. Preeminence
   To have first place

**THE PREEMINENCE OF CHRIST**
**BLOCK 5 - THEME 1 - LESSON 3 (147 OF 216)**
**QUESTIONS**

1. What percentage of Southern Baptist churches are struggling to continue their ministry?

2. List three reasons from this lesson why churches may struggle.

3. What can be the same reason for many different problems in the church and in individual lives?

4. What is the difference in the meaning of prominence and preeminence?

5. When we use the expression "the preeminence of Christ" what do we mean?

6. Who spoke "I am Alpha and Omega, the beginning and the end, the first and the last" and what is being said to us?

7. In your own life, would you say that Christ has no place at all, that he is prominent, or that he is preeminent?

8. What is Christ's purpose for the church and what did he accomplish to fulfill this purpose?

9. What is the Great Commission?

# 4. CHRIST'S LOVE FOR THE CHURCH

## THEME: CHRIST: THE HEAD OF THE BODY

BLOCK 5 - THEME 1 - LESSON 4

**LESSON AIM:** Share some of the ways Christ shows his love for the church.

**SCRIPTURE**: (Ephesians 5:21-33)

To be in love with someone is a wonderful thing. Most people begin to think about being in love as a young child. We observe our parents and older siblings and other adults in their relationships. Something within us longs to love and to be loved. We get girlfriends and boyfriends oftentimes while we are yet in elementary school. And we begin to set our eyes and our hearts at watch for that special someone whom we fully expect to come into our life one day.

When that special person arrives in our life, we enjoy a relationship unlike any other relationship we have with any other person on earth. It far surpasses the relationships we have with mothers and daddies, brothers and sisters, and with our closest friends. Among these relationships, we have no comparison for the love between a man and a woman. There is, however, a relationship to which it compares and this relationship is even greater than the one between a man and a woman. It is the relationship between Christ and his bride, the church. In fact, the relationship between Christ and the church is the model for our relationship with our spouse.

The Scripture passage for this lesson is the best marriage counseling information in the world. Those with troubled marriages and those who want to be the best kind of husband or the best kind of wife need only to read, study, learn, and apply these concepts to their marriage to have a blessed and lasting relationship. We find that the marriage relationship is a holy union and it thrives best when those who are in it treat it in terms of holiness. It is comparable to the individual Christian's relationship with Christ, and to Christ's relationship with the church. Like these relationships, in many ways, marriage is a kind of salvation: not from eternal damnation, but from loneliness, selfishness, and from all the things which seek to decay and destroy a marriage. In this model relationship between Christ and the church, Christ is like the husband, and the church is like the wife. We can take the things this text tells us about Christ and the church and apply them to our relationship with our spouse.

Let's note some things the text tells us about Christ and his love for the church. To begin with, we are reminded to observe the roles which each partner plays. Christ is the head of the church. We have already had an entire lesson on this point. He is also savior of the body. This is a reference to his love so deep that he laid down his life for his bride. Next we note the role of the church in submission to Christ as the body can do nothing without direction from the head. Herein lay the source of many of our problems in the church and in the home. When we reverse these roles, we create the problems.

This passage tells us three things in particular that Christ did and does to show his great love for the church. In the first place, he gave himself for the church. He gave up his own life in death on the cross to make this relationship a reality. There is no greater way to show or prove real love than this. Christ's death, however, was not the end of the story of his love. He took up his life again by the power of God and he draws us into this great love affair with himself.

We see in this passage that Christ gave himself for the church in order that he might do two other things. One, he gave himself for the church in order to prepare it for a relationship with him. He has sanctified the church, that is, he has chosen it and set it aside for himself. And, he is in the process of cleaning it up from all the dirt and damage that sin has caused. Two, he plans to present the church as a bride to himself: a perfect bride, beautiful and pure in every way.

While we are discussing these two things Christ is doing to and for the church, let's note a couple of important truths from them that we can apply to our life. Many people think they have to clean up their own life before coming to God. This is not possible. It is a useless activity which will end up taking them farther from God instead of bringing them closer to him. It is Christ's job to clean up the believing sinner. We need to but submit to his cleansing which comes through his blood that he shed for us and from the Word of God as we get it into our hearts. The other truth can be applied in our marriage relationship; now for those who are married, or later for those who are not married. We should see our spouse as Christ sees the church. At this time, the church is far from perfect. It has many areas in which to grow and mature. Yet Christ does not look at it as it is, but as it will become. Instead of noting and keeping score on all the ways our spouse may seem less than they are, we should look beyond this to a time when they will have grown past these issues as a result of our undying love for them over a period of time.

The other two things the text tells us about Christ's love for the church reveal how his love can heal the brokenness, smooth out the wrinkles, and release the glory of the bride. The second thing Christ does to show his love for the church is to nourish it. This means that he will bring it to maturity. This is what we call the process of sanctification. Christ is working to bring us to spiritual maturity. The word "nourish" also says something about how he will accomplish this. He will do it tenderly and gently. Even in times when it seems like he has crushed us from every possible angle, it will still be out of love and tender care.

Christ also shows his love for the church by cherishing it. This word means to sit on eggs until they hatch. This speaks of the longsuffering of Christ for us as we are sometimes as hard-headed as we are hard-hearted toward him. He stays with us and stays involved in the process, and is not turned away from his ultimate goal by our difficulties. It also speaks of warmth and of creating an environment from which life can emerge and grow and develop.

All these wonderful things are done for us as Christ shows his love for the church. He gave himself for us. He nourishes us. And he cherishes us. Have you responded to his love by believing upon him in your heart? If not, Please do so right now.

**CHRIST'S LOVE FOR THE CHURCH**
**BLOCK 5 - THEME 1 - LESSON 4 (148 OF 216)**
**LESSON OUTLINE**

**I CHRIST GAVE HIMSELF FOR THE CHURCH**
A. To prepare it for a relationship with him
B. To present it to himself as his bride

**II CHRIST NOURISHES THE CHURCH**
A. To nourish is to bring up to maturity
B. Christ nourishes us through the process of sanctification

**III CHRIST CHERISHES THE CHURCH**
A. Cherish means to sit on eggs until they hatch
B. This speaks of Christ's longsuffering with his people.

**SCRIPTURES TO BROADEN YOUR UNDERSTANDING**

1. Christ's love for us
   John 15:13

2. Christ died for us
   Romans 5:7-8

3. Husband and wife
   Genesis 2:20-25
   1 Peter 3:1-7

**LINES OF THEOLOGICAL CONNECTION**

1. ECCLESIOLOGY
   The church is the bride of Christ

2. CHRISTOLOGY
   Christ proved his love for the church at the cross

3. SOTERIOLOGY
   Sanctification

4. ANTHROPOLOGY
   The marriage relationship

**CHRIST'S LOVE FOR THE CHURCH**
**BLOCK 5 - THEME 1 - LESSON 4 (148 OF 216)**
**QUESTIONS**

1. What relationship mirrors the relationship between a husband and a wife?

2. In the model relationship between Christ and the church, what part is Christ like and what part is the church?

3. What three things does Christ do for the church?

4. Where can we go to find the best advice to help in our relationships in this life? How is it helpful?

5. How is marriage like salvation?

6. Why do you think some people think they have to clean up their life before coming to Christ?

7. Whose job is it to clean up the believing sinner? Why?

8. How do you think we can model Christ's love for the church in our marriage relationships?

9. What do you think our relationship with Christ should say about our commitment to our spouse?

# 5. CHRIST HAS TWO BODIES

## THEME: THE CHURCH: THE BODY OF CHRIST

BLOCK 5 - THEME 2 - LESSON 1

**LESSON AIM:** Show that Christ has two bodies; one physical, and one mystical.

**SCRIPTURE:** (Ephesians 1:22-23)

Many times, in our study of the Bible, we come across words or phrases which can have more than one meaning or application. We cannot assume that a word always means the same thing every time we encounter that word in the Bible. We have to go to the effort to determine which word was used in the original language, how it translates into English, and what it means for us today. This lesson provides a great example of this issue. When the Bible speaks of the body of Christ, there are two completely different things to which it may refer. We must keep the two meanings separate in our minds, and identify which body is spoken of if we are to understand the message God is communicating to us in his Word.

The Scriptures tell us that Christ has two bodies. One is the physical body that was given to him when he came into the world. Before the incarnation, Christ lived as does the Father and the Spirit; he was in spirit form. In other words, he did not have a visible human body like the bodies we have. When the time came for God to send his deliverer into the world, the Holy Ghost overshadowed Mary and she conceived the baby Jesus in her womb. The body of Jesus went through all the same growth process in the womb that all human beings go through. He progressed and grew through each stage of pre-natal development until finally, on that night in a cattle stable in Bethlehem, his physical body was born into the world.

In the physical body of Jesus, he experienced life in the same way as we experience it. He was a helpless infant, cared for by his earthly parents. He grew as a child, learned to read and write and to work. He learned the trade of his earth dad, Joseph, and worked as a carpenter. He knew what it was to be hot and cold, tired and weary, hungry and thirsty, and even grieved in his spirit and felt physical pain. He experienced all things in life that we experience so he would know how we feel when we experience life's good and bad. In this way, he learned to identify with us in our humanity.

The most important thing about the human body of Jesus is that he laid it down as a sacrifice for man on the cross. God required death as a penalty for sin. God would offer himself in death in the person of Jesus to satisfy his own penalty for sin. However, as God, he was unable to die. He had to make himself human in order to be able to die. Jesus, in his physical body, bore the torture and death of the cross that we might be saved. After his death, he arose from the dead and is alive today. For 40 days after the resurrection, Jesus showed himself alive to many people; to as many as 500 at one time. They saw him alive. They touched him and felt his physical body. They spoke with him. They ate meals with him. They were convinced that he was alive. Finally, they saw his body ascend into heaven and go out of sight. Today, Jesus lives in this same physical body, seated on the throne at the right hand of God in heaven. And, the Bible tells us that he is coming back to the earth in the future to rule the world. Yes, Jesus has a physical body, just like our body.

The Bible also tells us that Jesus has a second body. This body we might call his mystical body. Not mystical in the sense of magic or of the occult, but in the sense of being invisible, and yet seen at the same time. The mystical body of Christ is the church. The church is made up of believers in Christ who live during the time period between his resurrection and his return for the church. This group of believers is called in the Bible, the church, the body of Christ.

We become part of the body of Christ the instant we believe on Jesus for salvation. For people to believe on Jesus, someone has to share the good news of salvation in Christ with them. They hear the gospel and the Holy Spirit works in their heart to help them believe and to confess their belief in Christ. When a person believes, the Holy Spirit makes them a part of the body of Christ at that time.

The parts of the body of Christ are called *members* in the Bible. There is only one body, but it has many members. Each believer is a member of the body. As a member of the body, we have a place in the body specifically determined for us by God himself. From that place in the body, we are to live and function in the role we are to play in the body. In our physical bodies, each part has its own place. The hand works best when it is connected to the wrist; not if it is projecting from the middle of our upper back. In the same way, each member of the body of Christ has a place and a function to fulfill. The need is that we all might discover the particular place in which God has located us in his body, and the work he wants us to do from that place.

Part of what we are to do in our place as a member of the body is to be a connecting point for other members of the body and to pass nourishment to those parts with which we are directly connected. In this way, the body can be healthy and can grow as it should. When the members block the flow of nourishment by being out of place or stunted in their growth in some way, the rest of the body can suffer. When we all are in our place and doing our job, the body can be healthy and can do what God wants it to do in the world. Jesus can live in the body and continue his work to reach other people in the world who have not had the opportunity to hear his good news and believe on him and become a member of his body.

Although the body of Christ cannot be seen as a body the way we see our bodies, we can see it in a couple of different forms. We can see it in the form of a local church congregation, which we see in many places around our cities. And, we can see the body of Christ at work through the lives of individual Christians. By observing these two forms, we can see some of the many wonderful things that Christ is doing in the world today.

Jesus is still alive and well and at work throughout the world in our day and time. He lives in his body, the church. He wants to do the same things through this body that he did in his physical body while he walked on the earth. Are you a part of his body? Have you believed on Jesus for salvation? And, if so, have you discovered the place and role in his body that he wants you to fulfill?

**CHRIST HAS TWO BODIES**
**BLOCK 5 - THEME 2 - LESSON 1 (149 OF 216)**
**LESSON OUTLINE**

**I THE PHYSICAL BODY OF CHRIST**

A. The pre-incarnate Christ
B. The birth of Christ
C. Christ experienced life as we do in his physical body
D. Christ laid down his life as a sacrifice
E. Christ arose from the dead in his physical body
F. Christ is presently seated at God's right hand
G. Christ is coming again to the earth

**II THE MYSTICAL BODY OF CHRIST**

A. Invisible, yet visible
   1. The body is the church
   2. The church is made of members
   3. Each member has a function
B. Seeing the body at work
   1. The local church
   2. The individual Christian

**SCRIPTURES TO BROADEN YOUR UNDERSTANDING**

1. Jesus' conception in the womb of Mary
   Luke 1:26-56

2. The birth of the physical body of Jesus
   Luke 2:1-20

3. Things Jesus experienced in his human body
   * Hunger - Matthew 4:2
   * Thirst - John 4:7; 19:28
   * Fatigue - John 4:6
   * Love - John 11:5
   * Weeping - John 11:35
   * Testing - Matthew 4:1-11; Hebrews 4:15
   * Sorrow - Matthew 26:37
   * Death - Matthew 27:50
   * Resurrection - Matthew 28:1-6

4. Jesus was seen in his physical body after the resurrection
   Acts 1:3
   1 Corinthians 15:1-8

5. Jesus ascended to heaven in his physical body
   Acts 1:9-11

6. Jesus' future return to the earth in his physical body
   Revelation 19:11-16

7. Jesus' mystical body, the church
   Romans 12:4
   1 Corinthians 12:12-27
   Ephesians 4:4-16

**LINES OF THEOLOGICAL CONNECTION**

1. ECCLESIOLOGY
   The local church
   The individual believer

2. ANTHROPOLOGY
   Each believer has a specific purpose

3. CHRISTOLOGY
   The two bodies of Christ
   Indwelling
   The deity of Christ
   The humanity of Christ

4. ESCHATOLOGY
   The rapture
   The return of Christ
   The revelation of Christ

**LESSON GLOSSARY**

1. Ascend
   To rise upward

2. Congregation
   An assembly of persons, usually for worship

3. Mystical
   Characterized by mystery

**CHRIST HAS TWO BODIES**
**BLOCK 5 - THEME 2 - LESSON 1 (149 OF 216)**
**QUESTIONS**

1. What is the difference between the two bodies of Christ?

2. List some things Jesus experienced in his physical body.

3. Jesus experienced life as we experience it. How do you feel about the fact that Jesus knows how you feel when you experience unpleasant things in life?

4. Read Matthew chapters 26-28. What other characteristics of humanity can you pick out from this experience in the life of Jesus?

5. To be a part of the mystical body of Christ, the church, one must be a believer in Jesus Christ. Are you part of the body of Christ?

6. The Bible teaches that Jesus is coming back to the earth and will rule the world for 1,000 years. This is called the Millennial Reign of Christ. Christians will rule and reign with him in this kingdom. Have you given any thought to this future kingdom to come and to your role in it?

# 6. THREE PICTURES OF THE CHURCH

## THEME: THE CHURCH: THE BODY OF CHRIST

BLOCK 5 - THEME 2 - LESSON 2

**LESSON AIM**: Show three illustrations of the church in Ephesians.

**SCRIPTURE:** (Ephesians 1:23; 2:11-3:21; 5:21-33)

Communicating a message to another person is sometimes a difficult task. We do not always remember that communication is a two-way street and that all parties involved in the passing of information have to be on the same page if the message is to come across as it was intended. The person with the information feels that just because he has said the words from his mouth that the person who heard it understood it just as he intended it to be. This is not always the case. The person hearing the message has been conditioned to receive information in a certain way. All the information he receives passes through his personal information filtering process, making him receive information from a viewpoint perhaps other than that of the communicator. So, when a message is transmitted from one person to another, there are often two messages in the end; the message the communicator intended, and the message the hearer received. These are not always one and the same.

This idea is very important when it comes to Bible study. God is the person who has communicated a message in the Bible. The Bible is God's revelation of himself, his purpose, and his ways to man. This is why it is important to try to be sure of the message God intended to communicate as we read the Bible. This is known as Bible interpretation. Many times several people may read the same Bible passage and each one come up with a different interpretation. This should not be. There is one interpretation but there may be many ways to apply it in our lives. The interpretation is not what the reader wants it to be but what God meant it to be when he recorded his message in the Bible. There are rules we have to follow when it comes to interpreting the Scriptures to do our best to get the message God intended us to receive. The study of theology which is concerned with the rules of Bible interpretation is called hermeneutics.

Jesus was a careful communicator when he spoke to his listeners. He wanted to leave as little room as possible for his message to be misunderstood. One of the things he did to help get his point across was to use illustrations to enhance his message. His illustrations are called parables, and there are many of them in his messages. The parables, or illustrations, gave his listeners a common connection to his message through something with which they were already familiar. On one occasion when Jesus spoke about worry and anxiety, he told the people to think about the birds, for example. They do not plant and harvest or store food into barns, yet God takes care of them. He went on to say if God takes care of the birds he will surely take care of you. These illustrations helped get his point across to his audience and they still help us today as we read and seek to understand God's message to us in our day from the Bible.

When writing of the church in the book of Ephesians Paul also used illustrations to get his point across to his readers. The primary message in this short letter is of the church and its relationship to Jesus Christ. Paul uses three illustrations to communicate his message of the church. He says the church is like a body, a building, and a bride. From these illustrations, we can learn much about the church and how important it is to God, and therefore how important it should be to us.

First, Paul says the church is like a body. What he is saying is that Jesus operates in the world just like we do. We live inside a body and everything we do, we have to do through our body. In the same way Jesus lives in his body, the church. He works through the church to do his work of reaching the lost and the unreached with his gospel. Christ is the head of the body and the body receives its orders from the head. Through a system of nerves, our brain communicates its commands to all the parts of our body, telling them what to do. This is a great picture of how we, as members of the body of Christ, should receive our orders from Christ who is the head of the body and obey his commands.

Paul also illustrates the church as a building. This is a great illustration. Think of the building you live in. It has a foundation on which it rests. It has framework which gives it shape, structure and strength. Everything else is supported by the framework. It has a function; it houses your family. In your house, you have shelter from the elements and you have a place to live, grow up and cultivate your relationships with your family. The church as a building works in the same way. In the same way that each one of us is a member of the body of Christ, we are also members of the building of Christ. We have a specific place in the building and a specific job to do in that place. The smallest member of a building has an important role to play just like the larger members. Remove all the nails from a building and see how long it can stand. The small little nail plays a key role. Each one of us has a key role in the building of God called the church.

The church is also called a bride. Little girls dream of being a bride one day. At some point in a boy's life, he begins to think about girls and about having a wife of his own. God made us to think in this way because his plan is for us to reproduce and fill the earth with people who will fellowship with God. There is nothing more beautiful and nothing which speaks of tender love than a bride on her wedding day. The church is the bride of Christ. Just as a man loves and cares for his bride, Christ loves and cares for the church. In the same way that each one of us is a member of the body and building of Christ, we are also a member of the bride of Christ. He loves and cares for us in this wonderful, tender, and caring way.

Through these three illustrations, we can see something more of our relationship with Christ. As a body, we see that Christ lives *in* us and wants to live *through* us to the ends of the earth until the end of time. As a building, we see that Christ wants to live *with* us. The church is his dwelling place where he can live with his people. And, through the bride, we can see that God lives *for* us. He loved the bride and gave himself for the church. These pictures which help us understand how important the church is to God also communicate to us some of the many ways God has shown his love and care for us. May the church be as important to us as it is to God.

**THREE PICTURES OF THE CHURCH**
**BLOCK 5 - THEME 2 - LESSON 2 (150 OF 216)**
**LESSON OUTLINE**

**I A BODY**
A. Christ has a body
B. Christ works through his body

**II A BUILDING**
A. A foundation
B. A framework
C. A function

**III A BRIDE**
Each illustrates the other
A. Christ and his love for the church
B. A husband and his love for his wife

**SCRIPTURES TO BROADEN YOUR UNDERSTANDING**

1. God communicated his message to man
   2 Peter 1:19-21

2. The Holy Spirit helps us understand the message God has communicated to us
   1 Corinthians 2
   1 John 2:20,27

3. The church as a body, building, and bride
   Ephesians (Entire book)

**LINES OF THEOLOGICAL CONNECTION**

1. BIBLIOLOGY
   Revelation
   Inspiration
   Hermeneutics
   Communicating God's Word
   Application of God's Word

2. ECCLESIOLOGY
   The body of Christ

3. CHRISTOLOGY
   Christ's love for the church

**LESSON GLOSSARY**

1. Hermeneutics
   The principles of Bible interpretation

2. Exegesis
   An interpretation of a text

3. Parable
   A simple story used to illustrate a truth

**THREE PICTURES OF THE CHURCH**
**BLOCK 5 - THEME 2 - LESSON 2 (150 OF 216)**
**QUESTIONS**

1. What is the theological study of the principles of Bible interpretation called?

2. List Paul's three illustrations of the church.

3. What role do you play in the body of Christ?

4. Every role in the body of Christ is important. What benefit does your role provide to the church?

5. Two specific ways that we show our respect for the church are by our regular attendance and support. Are you a faithful attender and supporter of the local church?

## 7. BELIEVERS HAVE A SPECIFIC PLACE IN THE BODY OF CHRIST

## THEME: THE CHURCH: THE BODY OF CHRIST

BLOCK 5 - THEME 2 - LESSON 3

**LESSON AIM:** Show how God has chosen our place in the body of Christ.

**SCRIPTURE:** (1 Corinthians 12:12-27) Key Verse 18

*But now hath God set the members every one of them in the body, as it hath pleased him.*

During the time in which we live, God is about the work of building the church. The church is made up primarily of Gentiles, that is, people from ethnic groups other than the Jews. Some Jews have also believed on Christ, but as a nation, they do not accept that Jesus is the Messiah that God promised to send into the world to deliver them. Because of their unbelief, God has caused them to have a spiritual blindness toward Christ at this time. God will, of course, continue his plans toward Israel. But for now, he is calling out the church and using it to do the job that he had wanted Israel to do.

Your life will begin to make much more sense in the world if you will get a grasp on this one important truth of the Scriptures: the church is the context for your life in the world as a believer in Christ. The problem many Christians have, and the reason for so much frustration in their life after they believe is that they are trying to live a dual life. They are trying to live as a part of the church, and are trying to continue to live in the world at the same time. By living in the world, I mean that they want to continue to indulge in the sins, desires and pleasures of the flesh instead of coming out from these things to live a holy life before God. Living this way is evidence of a heart not fully committed to God. This is a way of life in which God is not pleased. When we believe on Christ, God places us in the body of Christ, the church. After this point, the church should be the context for our life. Every decision we make from now on should be made based on how it will help or hinder the church of which we are a part. Living in the context of the church will help us to see and live for something much bigger than ourselves.

Our key verse for this lesson tells us that God has set us in the body as it pleased him. In other words, he picked the very place in the body and the part that each one of us will play as a part of the church. This part is not something we determine on our own. We are to seek to discover it, and when we do, we are to live to fulfill our work in and from that place. Our place in the body affords us many blessings, four of which we want to consider now.

To have a place in the body of Christ chosen for us by God himself gives us a place in which to belong. I can remember as a teenager having a strong desire to belong to something; something bigger than myself; something in which I could find meaning for life. I eventually came to realize that the church is the one and only place in the world in which we can find ultimate satisfaction and belonging. We may join a civic club, or we may be a member of the military, or we may play on a sports team, or any one of a thousand other pursuits, yet in these we can never find what we have as a member of the body of Christ. It is not necessarily wrong to be a part of things like this, unless we let those things become a substitute for the part we are to play in the church. The church is truly a place of belonging. When we finally discover our place in it and settle into it, it is like coming home after a long and exhausting journey.

As we discover and begin to fulfill our role in the church, we also realize how much we are needed by others. As a member of the body with a specific role to play, we find that we can make a contribution to the ministry and work of the church. This is so important because it helps us transition from being a taker, to being a giver. Some people always want to receive things from the church and never contribute to it. As a member of the body, we have a function, and as we perform that function, we contribute to the health and work of the body. This gives us a fair stock in rejoicing over the accomplishments the body achieves as a whole. By fulfilling our role, we contribute unity and wholeness to the body. As all the parts of the body work together for the common goal God has given us, division of the body is prevented. This unity is a need that we all can contribute to as we fulfill our place in the church.

Our place in the body also gives us a purpose for which to live. These first three blessings we have mentioned are core needs that every person on earth has. We all have the need to belong, to be needed, and to have a purpose for our life. These things are those which people are seeking in so many ways and in so many places. It is interesting that God has designed a way to meet all of these needs through giving us a place in his body, the church. This should underscore the importance of the church in our lives yet again.

We stated that our place in the body gives us purpose. Think of the parts of your physical body and how their place determines their purpose. Our hands for example, with the individual fingers and means of motion and mobility are at the end of our forearms, the best place they could possibly be in order to do all that they do. They pick up things, catch things, push and pull things, and so many other functions that the whole body needs. They would not be as useful in any other place in the body. We are just that way. God has chosen our place in the body. Our place defines our function. And our function is our purpose in life. To try to live in any other place or for any other purpose is to forfeit all opportunity to live the life God wants us to live.

Our place in the body also is a unique place. No other person can come to our place and fulfill our part. Neither can we fulfill the part of others. Our uniqueness shows our value to the body. We have a unique place and role to fill, and so do all other members of the body of Christ. And the best part is, there is room for all of us in the body. We are not to think of our place and role as the best or most important part. Each part is in a unique place and has job to do that only it can do. To find and fulfill this place is the quest of life itself.

As a member of the body of Christ, you are in a place that God himself chose just for you. This fact alone is a wonderful thought and blessing. But it also brings with it many other blessings. Seek to discover that place in the body of Christ that God has hand-picked for you. You will never find peace and satisfaction in life until you do.

**BELIEVERS HAVE A SPECIFIC PLACE IN THE BODY OF CHRIST**
**BLOCK 5 - THEME 2 - LESSON 3 (151 OF 216)**
**LESSON OUTLINE**

**I WE HAVE A PLACE IN WHICH TO BELONG**
- A. People desire to have belonging
- B. Believers find belonging in the church

**II WE ARE NEEDED BY OTHERS**
- A. We make a contribution to the ministry
- B. We help to create unity in the body of Christ

**III WE HAVE A PURPOSE FOR WHICH TO LIVE**
- A. Place defines function
- B. Function reveals purpose

**IV WE HAVE A UNIQUE PLACE IN THE BODY OF CHRIST**
- A. It is solely ours
- B. It shows our value to the body
- C. There is room for all of us in the body of Christ

**SCRIPTURES TO BROADEN YOUR UNDERSTANDING**
1. The present blindness of Israel
   Romans 11:7, 25
   2 Corinthians 3:12-18

2. Israel's present position
   Matthew 23:37-39
   1 Thessalonians 2:14-16

3. Your spiritual gift equips you to fulfill your role in the body of Christ
   Romans 12

**LINES OF THEOLOGICAL CONNECTION**
1. ANTHROPOLOGY
   Self-worth

2. ECCLESIOLOGY
   Function in the body of Christ
   Spiritual gifts
   Unity in the church

**BELIEVERS HAVE A SPECIFIC PLACE IN THE BODY OF CHRIST**
**BLOCK 5 - THEME 2 - LESSON 3 (151 OF 216)**
**QUESTIONS**

1. What is a Gentile?

2. What great truth do we need to grasp as a Christian?

3. What source of frustration hinders us from living in the context of the church?

4. Do you struggle with this frustration? Explain.

5. What is indicated when a Christian continually gives in to this frustration?

6. What will it mean for the church to be the context for your life?

7. What does it mean to you that God has selected a specific place in his body just for you?

8. List four blessings of having a place in the body of Christ.

9. What is your place in the body of Christ?

## 8. THE CHURCH IS TO LIVE FOR THE GLORY OF GOD

## THEME: THE CHURCH: THE BODY OF CHRIST

BLOCK 5 - THEME 2 - LESSON 4

**LESSON AIM:** Show that the church is to live to bring glory to God in all that we do.

**SCRIPTURE:** (Ephesians 3:20-21)

"*Now unto him that is able to do exceeding abundantly above all that we ask or think, according to the power that worketh in us, Unto him be glory in the church by Christ Jesus throughout all ages, world without end. Amen*"

The Bible tells us how important the church is to God. He loved it and gave himself for it. It is his body, his building and his bride. It should be important to every Christian as well. He placed us in his body in a specific place and gave us a specific job to do. From our place, and through our job, or purpose, we are to bring glory to God in all that we do.

From our focal passage, the new or shallow Christian might think that God is telling us that we can ask for anything whatsoever and God will give it to us. In itself, this is not exactly true. Our asking has conditions upon it. We must recognize them if we are to ask properly and to expect our asking to be answered by God. James told us that we do not have the things we ask for either because we do not ask at all, or we ask for it for the wrong reasons. We are to ask for and do those things which will bring glory to God. Let's note three conditions placed upon our asking which will help us ask for the things which will glorify God.

First, we are to ask for things which are in accordance with the purpose of God. While this is not specifically stated in this particular passage, it is understood. Paul began this letter by telling us that we need to see things from God's point of view. And the very first thing Paul mentioned that we need to see from God's perspective is his purpose in our life. The fallen, fleshly nature wants to have its own way. This can carry over into our Christian life if we are not careful. The thing God wants and the thing to which we have to surrender is the purpose of God. Within the purpose of God, we are free and encouraged to ask for anything whatsoever that is in line with God's purpose for our life. He wants us to have those things and he is ready to give them to us, but he first wants us to want what he wants.

It is not a problem for God to do the things for which we ask. He is not only able to do them, but he is able to do them exceeding abundantly above all that we ask or think. This is another reason God wants us to ask within his purpose. When we think through a plan for ministry and working for the Lord, we should think our highest and best thoughts. We should ask for things that are impossible to us. We should ask for things which will increase our influence farther around the world. We should dream our wildest dreams for service and ministry within God's purpose. When we do, God is able to do even more than we have thought of or hoped for. He wants to do these things for us, but the condition is that we ask for those things which are within his purpose. If we want and do the things which are within his purpose, we will be assured that God will be glorified through our life and through the things that we do for him.

The next thing Paul mentions that conditions our asking and whether or not we bring glory to God is the power of God that is working in our life. We cannot work in the flesh and expect to please and glorify God. We must work in the Spirit. To work in the Spirit is to be empowered by God, the Holy Spirit, who works in and through us as we work for God. If God's Spirit is unhindered in our life by the flesh and sin, he is free to do the things he wants to do through us. We should make it a daily point to be sure we have nothing in our life which will short-circuit the work of the Holy Spirit. We need to draw near to God and resist the devil and walk in the power of the Holy Ghost. Galatians chapter 5 tells us how we can know the difference between living in the flesh and living in the Spirit. If the Spirit is in control of our life and we are working in the power of the Lord, God is pleased to give us the things for which we ask. He will not allow us to have his blessing in order to consume it upon our own fleshly and sinful lusts.

If we are to bring glory to God, we are to ask for things which are within the purpose of God. The power of God must be free in our life to work toward God's purpose. The last thing Paul names which conditions our asking is our perspective. We see this in verse 21 when he says that the church is to glorify God through Jesus Christ, throughout all ages, world without end. God is teaching us here again that our vision is to be both global and generational. God wants our lives to make an impact in the world. We should intentionally work to make our influence felt and our presence known in other places around the world, not only in the location in which we live. We have to think of ways to do this, and we have to put our ideas to work if this is going to happen. We cannot simply sit down and do nothing and hope that our territories will be enlarged. We have to work to make it happen. A good question to continually present to ourselves is this, "Who knows my name in at least one other country in the world?" If we will ask this question and work to know and be known by others in other places, we will achieve some measure of impact in the world and this will bring glory to God.

God also wants our impact to be felt in a generational way. That is, he wants us to live now in such a way that will impact the lives of people who will live on the earth in the future. We can do this by making disciples as Jesus commanded among our families and among others. Our family is probably our best opportunity to achieve a generational impact. As we disciple our children, they can disciple our grandchildren, and so on. King David is a great example of a man whose life continued to make an impact in his family and among other people even after his death. This is the scope of impact that God wants all of his people to have. We can live in such a way as to increase our influence in the world for time to come. This brings glory to God.

Christians, who are a part of the body of Christ, the church, are to live not for themselves but for the glory of God. We can do this when we pursue God's purpose, live out of his power, and live with a perspective that increases and ensures our impact in the world into the future. When God is glorified in this way, he is pleased to give us the things for which we ask under these conditions.

**THE CHURCH IS TO LIVE FOR THE GLORY OF GOD**
**BLOCK 5 - THEME 2 - LESSON 4 (152 OF 216)**
**LESSON OUTLINE**

Three conditions for asking in prayer

**I ASK ACCORDING TO GOD'S PURPOSE**
A. We must want what God wants
B. God can exceed our asking and thinking

**II ASK IN ACCORD WITH THE POWER OF GOD**
A. Resist the flesh
B. Walk in the Spirit

**III ASK WITH A PERSPECTIVE TOWARD THE FUTURE**
A. Global vision
B. Generational vision

**SCRIPTURES TO BROADEN YOUR UNDERSTANDING**

1. Jesus lived to glorify God
   John 17:4

2. War between the flesh and the spirit
   Galatians 5:16-6:1

3. Prayer for purpose, perspective, and power
   Ephesians 1:15-23

4. Asking in prayer
   Matthew 7:7-12
   John 14:13-15
   James 4

5. God's power in our life
   Ephesians 1:19

**LINES OF THEOLOGICAL CONNECTION**

1. DISCIPLE-MAKING
   World vision
   Global impact
   Generational impact

2. DOCTRINE OF PRAYER
   Asking correctly

3. INCARNATION
   God lives in us and through us

**THE CHURCH IS TO LIVE FOR THE GLORY OF GOD**
**BLOCK 5 - THEME 2 - LESSON 4 (152 OF 216)**
**QUESTIONS**

1. What is our chief aim in life?

2. From this lesson, list the three conditions for our asking in prayer.

3. Do you ask God for things outside the scope of these conditions?

4. Can you give an example of how God answered prayer when you prayed under these conditions?

5. Are you beginning to make any plans to help you make an impact in the world for the glory of God?

6. Do you think the way you live your life brings glory to God? In what ways?

7. Does anyone in another country know your name? What country?

8. Explain how selfishness in our lives can hinder the answer to our prayers.

# 9. THE CHURCH IS A MYSTERY

## THEME: THE CHURCH IN THE BIBLE

BLOCK 5 - THEME 3 - LESSON 1

**LESSON AIM:** Show that the church was a secret kept by God throughout history.

**SCRIPTURE:** (Ephesians 3:1-6)

4 *Whereby, when ye read, ye may understand my knowledge in the mystery of Christ)*
5 *Which in other ages was not made known unto the sons of men, as it is now revealed*
*unto his holy apostles and prophets by the Spirit;* 6 *That the Gentiles should be fellow-*
*heirs, and of the same body, and partakers of his promise in Christ by the gospel:*

We have seen by now that the church is very precious to the Lord Jesus Christ. It has been a part of the plan of God from the very beginning. However, God chose not to make this information known until just the right time in history. Hints of it were all around in the Old Testament but neither Israel nor her prophets understood to the full extent how God would include all peoples of the world in his work of global evangelization. This, God kept a secret all the way up to about 2,000 years ago when the church came into existence.

A secret like this is called a mystery in the Bible. There are three great mysteries named in the Bible and they all have to do with God's salvation and the preaching of the gospel to all people. The first mystery is called the blindness of Israel.

We should recall the things God said to Abraham when he called him for his purpose back in Genesis 12. He said that all peoples of the earth would be blessed through Abraham's offspring. God called Abraham and made a great nation of his people, the Jews, and they were to take the message of the glory of God to all peoples of the earth. The Jews are called God's chosen people for this reason. He chose them to evangelize the world. Somewhere along the line, Israel lost sight of their purpose and turned their eyes upon themselves. Instead of being God's favored people who were to gather in the fallen from all nations, they soon began to act as if they were God's favorite people out of all the families of the earth. This caused them to hoard the blessings of God instead of sharing them with others. Not long after abandoning their purpose, they soon turned their hearts away from God altogether. For this reason, God struck them with spiritual blindness for a period of time. As a result of this, the Jews as a whole do not recognize Jesus as the Messiah of the world, and their privilege of taking the good news about Christ to all peoples has been taken away from them and given to another group.

This is where the second great mystery comes into the story. In fact, the second mystery is a mystery within a mystery. The first part of this dual mystery is that the Gentiles would be fellow-heirs with Israel in the gospel. Paul says it like this in Ephesians 3:6: *That the Gentiles should be fellow-heirs, and of the same body, and partakers of his promise in Christ by the gospel.*

This again goes back to the promise God made to Abraham. Even then, the seeds of this plan were there. By way of the progressive revelation of God, we learn in the New Testament that all of those from all people groups in the world who would believe on Jesus Christ would be counted as one of the children of Abraham. From Jew and Gentile, God brought a single body into being and called it the church. This was the secret that God kept in his heart until it was time to reveal it.

What caused it to be the right time to reveal this secret? The history of the Jews is one of hard hearts and stiff necks. They have a record of rebellion against God to the point of abandonment. Time after time, God worked to chasten them and bring them back to himself that his purpose to save some from all nations could be accomplished. They continually refused his presence and work in their lives. They killed the prophets that God sent to them to try to warn and turn their hearts back to God. Eventually, they even killed the very one whom God sent to deliver them and all others from sin. After the resurrection of Jesus from the dead, God gave them a last chance to acknowledge Jesus as the Christ and receive the kingdom he wanted to bring in. To this offer of the kingdom they made a three-fold refusal which is documented in the book of Acts. Upon their final refusal to be and do what God wanted them to be and do, God revealed his secret to the world: the church. Paul noted this in Acts 28:25-28:

[25] *And when they agreed not among themselves, they departed, after that Paul had spoken one word, Well spake the Holy Ghost by Esaias the prophet unto our fathers,*
[26] *Saying, Go unto this people, and say, Hearing ye shall hear, and shall not understand; and seeing ye shall see, and not perceive:* [27] *For the heart of this people is waxed gross, and their ears are dull of hearing, and their eyes have they closed; lest they should see with their eyes, and hear with their ears, and understand with their heart, and should be converted, and I should heal them.* [28] *Be it known therefore unto you, that the salvation of God is sent unto the Gentiles, and that they will hear it.*

During the age of the church, God has taken away the privilege of evangelizing the world from the Jews and has given it to the church which is a body made mostly of Gentile believers and of some believing Jews. The church was another of God's great secrets kept in his heart from the foundation of the world and revealed in due time.

Within the mystery of the church is another mystery of which Paul speaks in Colossians chapter one. This great secret which God revealed is that Christ would personally live in every believer who is a part of the church. This secret has tremendous effects in many areas, two of which we will name. The first area is in the life of the believer. What does it mean to you to know that Jesus lives within you? It means that he is always with us and never leaves us. He is with us in all circumstances and places. He is there to guide and protect and to love. So many benefits are ours because Jesus dwells within us.

A second area of benefit, of course, is what this means to our adversary, the devil. Instead of trying to defeat one Jesus, he has to contend with millions of people on earth who each have Jesus living within them. This makes it impossible for him to ultimately defeat the church, even though he can inflict very serious damage upon it.

By this act of the indwelling Jesus in each believer, God has made it impossible for the gates of hell to ever prevail against the church of the living God.

At a specified time in the future, God is going to remove the church from the world. He will remove the blindness from the heart of Israel and once again give them the assignment of finishing the task of evangelizing the world. The job will be completed at that time, but it will be under the most horrendous circumstances imaginable. God will bring Israel's heart back to him and they will admit that Jesus is their Messiah. Jesus will rule them and the world from Jerusalem for 1,000 years. God's purpose will at last be done on the earth. Thank God for his marvelous plan and for allowing us to have a part in it as a member of his church.

**THE CHURCH IS A MYSTERY**
**BLOCK 5 - THEME 3 - LESSON 1 (153 OF 216)**
**LESSON OUTLINE**

Bible mysteries:

**I THE BLINDNESS OF ISRAEL**

A. Chosen to evangelize the world
B. Refused to fulfill their assignment
C. Lost opportunity

**II THE CHURCH**

A. Gentiles are fellow-heirs with the Jews
B. The indwelling Christ
   1. Christ lives within us
   2. The devil has a large enemy in the church to contend with

**SCRIPTURES TO BROADEN YOUR UNDERSTANDING**

1. The church was a secret
   Romans 16:25

2. Three groupings of the world's population
   1 Corinthians 10:32

3. Israel's present condition
   1 Thessalonians 2:14-16

**LINES OF THEOLOGICAL CONNECTION**

1. SOTERIOLOGY
   The blindness of Israel
   The church

2. ESCHATOLOGY
   The second coming of Christ
   The tribulation and the great tribulation
   Israel will finish the task of world evangelization
   The millennial reign of Christ

LESSON GLOSSARY

1. Progressive
   Advancing; unfolding

**THE CHURCH IS A MYSTERY**
**BLOCK 5 - THEME 3 - LESSON 1 (153 OF 216)**
**QUESTIONS**

1. What people make up the church?

2. List three secrets revealed in the New Testament.

3. Why was Israel blinded?

4. What is another word for a mystery?

5. Why are the Jews called God's chosen people?

6. Do you believe on Christ in your heart?

7. Do you tell others about Christ and how they can have a relationship with him?

# 10. THE CHURCH IS BORN

## THEME: THE CHURCH IN THE BIBLE

BLOCK 5 - THEME 3 - LESSON 2

**LESSON AIM:** Show the entry of the church in the plans of God for the world.

**SCRIPTURE:** (Acts 28:28)

*"Be it known therefore unto you, that the salvation of God is sent unto the Gentiles, and that they will hear it."*

From the time of God's call to Abraham, God's plan was to bring forth a nation of people that he could use to take his message of rescue and deliverance through Christ to all the peoples of the world. The nation he chose to use was the Jews, the descendants of Abraham. God spent centuries preparing them for their assignment, yet all the while, their hearts were not fully after the Lord. He gave them his laws and all of the illustrations they would ever need to share the gospel message. He sent prophets to point them toward God and call them back to him. Eventually, God sent the Messiah that he had promised but the Jews refused him and the offer of his kingdom. They called out for his execution and got it. Thankfully, this was not the end of the story. The Messiah arose from the dead, still intending to continue his ministry and message of salvation to the world.

In the book of Acts, we have two major things taking place at the same time. In each one of them, we can see the mercy and longsuffering of God as he continues to work his plan even though man is so reluctant to go along with him. The first thing we see is God offering the kingdom and the evangelistic assignment to the Jews again, even after they had crucified Jesus. The unfolding story of the book of Acts, covering a period of about thirty years, reveals three specific times when the Jews refused the Messiah and his kingdom. The first refusal came in Acts 7:54-60 by the Jews in Jerusalem marked by the stoning of Stephen. The second refusal occurred in Acts 22:20-23 by the Jews who were dispersed throughout the regions. The third and last refusal was made all the way to the city of Rome by the leaders of the Jews at the farthest extent of the gospel advance at the time. We read of this in Acts 28:28. In spite of the fact that the Jews had always been a hard-hearted and stiff-necked people, and had killed the Messiah, God on three occasions offered his kingdom and assignment to them and three more times they refused. For this final refusal, God caused them as a nation to be stricken with spiritual blindness. This is the spiritual condition of the Jews at the present time.

At the same time that God was offering the Jews three more opportunities to join him in his work of world evangelism, and receiving three more refusals from his chosen people, he was at work to develop another group to take their place in the work for a period of time. This group is called the church.

The church is made up of believers in Christ, regardless of their ethnicity. This is what Paul meant when he said that salvation is sent to the Gentiles. All the while the Jews were refusing God's calling, God was working to continue his mission to the world through those who believed on him from every nation.

One meaning of the word *church* is assembly. As people from other ethnic groups began to hear the gospel and believe on Jesus, they began to assemble themselves for the purpose of worshipping God and doing the work of the ministry. This work included evangelizing others with the message of the gospel and making disciples of the evangelized. Local churches began to be planted in cities throughout the world. God prepared a man named Paul to be the key leader in the establishment, development, and extension of the church in its early days. He and his partners in the work planted churches in many places. He worked to train men to be the pastors of the churches to lead them to do the work of the Lord. He wrote letters of instruction and encouragement to them which God intended to be used as Holy Scriptures. We have these letters in our Bibles today. We still read them and use them with the help of the Holy Spirit to guide us in the work that we do through the church.

Churches today, 2,000 years after Paul established the first ones, still have the same purpose. God wants the church to work with him in the mission of getting the gospel of the Lord Jesus Christ to the people groups of the world who have not yet heard the story of God's salvation. Churches still need pastors to lead them into this mission. God is still calling men to be pastors and to plant churches where the church does not exist. These places are everywhere from large cities of modern countries like the United States, to small, remote, and unknown villages deep in the jungles of other continents.

God is also calling men and women to serve him through the church in various ways. There are other callings besides pastor which God may extend to his followers. Some Christians feel a call to work in the ministry of children, or youth, or single adults, or senior adults, or in many other ways. Some feel a call to music ministry, or maybe even to missionary service in another country. Some feel a call to a certain people group. The world is wide open, and the needs are abounding, and the possibilities are endless when it comes to what you can do in the service of the Lord.

As a member of the Lord's church through salvation in Jesus, we all have an obligation to determine how God wants to use us in his service. We need to explore the possibilities. We need to educate ourselves on the agencies that are available through which to work. Our Southern Baptist Denomination has two particular agencies which prepare and send Christian workers and missionaries to many places around the world. One agency, the North American Mission Board, works to send people to plant the church and make disciples within the continent of North America. The second agency, the International Mission Board, sends workers into other countries for mission work. There are also many other mission sending agencies which do the same. If you think God is drawing you in this direction with your life, you should begin to research these agencies, asking God what is his will for your life. He will lead you to the place where he wants you to be, and he will reveal the pathway he wants you to follow in order to get there.

While it is not God's plan that every Christian go to another country to share the gospel with other nations, it is his will that every Christian be engaged in this ministry where we are. All around us are people who do not know the Lord and have not heard a clear presentation of the gospel. All of us can do this ministry in our own homes, in our own schools, in our own communities, and on our jobs. God has brought the people of the world to our doorsteps. And we all can be a global witness for Christ as a member of his church without even leaving our hometown.

We read in the book of Acts how God brought the church into being. We read how the church, for a time, has taken the Jews place in taking the gospel to the world. The church today has the same mission. We all need to join in the work through the church while we have the opportunity. One day, God is going to remove the church from the world and will give Israel a last opportunity to do the work of evangelism. At that time, they will do it. Until then, it is up to us as members of the church to join with God in preaching the glad tidings of the kingdom to all nations. What does God want you to do to be a part of this work through his church?

**THE CHURCH IS BORN**
**BLOCK 5 - THEME 3 - LESSON 2 (154 OF 216)**
**LESSON OUTLINE**

**I ISRAEL REFUSES THE KINGDOM OF CHRIST**

A. By the Jews in Jerusalem at the stoning of Stephen
B. By the Jews of the dispersion
C. By the Jews in Rome

**II THE RISE OF THE CHURCH**

A. The work of the church
   1. Evangelism
   2. Disciple-making
B. Paul's role in the early church
C. Your role in the church today

**SCRIPTURES TO BROADEN YOUR UNDERSTANDING**

1. The great commission
   Matthew 28:18-20

2. God's calling
   Romans 8:28-30
   Ephesians 2:10

**LINES OF THEOLOGICAL CONNECTION**

1. THE DOCTRINE OF THE SCRIPTURES
   Paul's writings in the New Testament

2. THE DOCTRINE OF THE CHURCH
   Paul's missionary journeys
   The establishment of the first churches
   The early development of the church

**LESSON GLOSSARY**

1. Dispersed
   Scattered

**THE CHURCH IS BORN**
**BLOCK 5 - THEME 3 - LESSON 2 (154 OF 216)**
**QUESTIONS**

1. What two major events take place in the book of Acts?

2. What is another word for a church?

3. What is the two-fold work of the church?

4. What is the difference between the two works mentioned in the previous question?

5. Who was the key leader in the church in its early days?

6. God calls people to work for his church. Have you ever considered what God may be calling you to do in and for his church?

7. What are the two sending agencies of the Southern Baptist Convention?

8. Use the internet to research other mission agencies. Try to see if one of them offers a career that you may be interested in. What is it?

# 11. THE CHURCH MULTIPLIED

## THEME: THE CHURCH IN THE BIBLE

BLOCK 5 - THEME 3 - LESSON 3

**LESSON AIM:** Show the beginning of the multiplication of the church.

**SCRIPTURE:** (Acts 9:31)

*"Then had the churches rest throughout all Judaea and Galilee and Samaria, and were edified; and walking in the fear of the Lord, and in the comfort of the Holy Ghost, were multiplied."*

I love numbers. Numbers tell a story. A wise person will regularly observe the numbers and listen to the story they are telling. For example, if you balance your check book on a weekly basis, you can clearly see where your money is going and if you have any money left in the bank. The numbers will tell you if your present job brings in enough money to sustain your lifestyle, or if you need a second job, or perhaps a better job altogether. The numbers will tell you if you are making enough money but you are spending too much and you need to reign in your spending habits. Learn to listen to the numbers and to the story they are telling.

As a Christian, there are many numbers that we need to keep an eye upon. There are, however, two numbers that we need to look at regularly. These two numbers are the world's population and the world-wide growth of the church. In the book of Acts, we see the numbers of the early growth of the church. When the book of Acts opened, there were 120 people in the upper room waiting on the promise of the Father to empower them with the Holy Spirit. By the second chapter, there are more than 3,000 of them in Jerusalem. So, we see the church beginning to take off in her initial days of existence.

More than the actual numbers, we should note the method of acquiring the numbers and the development of that method. To begin with, souls were added to the church. Peter preached a fabulous message in the power of the Holy Spirit and 3,000 people came to the Lord in one day. The text says they were *added* to the church. All the way back in the book of Genesis, we learned that God has given man the command to multiply. Multiplication is a faster method of addition. If we are content to add to the church, we will not be able to keep pace with the growth of the population of the world. For this reason, Jesus left us a strategy for multiplication in our disciple-making ministry. The church has to multiply, first to be obedient to the Lord, and second, to try to not be so far behind in reaching the world with the gospel.

When we come to the sixth chapter of Acts, we see the disciples being multiplied. This is what the Lord wants for his church. He has commanded and commissioned each believer to multiply disciples. This is the mission in which every Christian should be engaged. The Bible tells us that we have everything we need in order to accomplish this command. God has given us this purpose. He has given us the grace, or the empowerment and resources to achieve the purpose of multiplying disciples. And, as we said, Jesus left us an example and a method to follow. There is absolutely no excuse for a Christian to not multiply disciples. There are really only two reasons why a Christian does not multiply. Either he does not know the Lord's method of multiplication, or, he simply is disobedient to do it.

The next step we see in the development of the numbers in the early church is that eventually, the churches began to multiply also. In the same way that individual Christians are to multiply, churches should also multiply other congregations. The multiplication of individual disciples and the multiplication of congregations are the two most important things a church can do. Many churches with a long history of existence have done little to no multiplication of either one of these. Some of these churches are flourishing and seem to have it all together. Some of them are in decline and are dying, if not already dead. A church can be dead without realizing it. People can continue to gather, the offerings can be good, the bills can be paid, but the church is dead or dying because it is not obeying the Lord's command to multiply. It is when we obey the commission to make and multiply disciples, which includes congregations of disciples, that the Lord has promised to be with us as we carry out his mission to the world. This then, becomes the measurement of whether or not a church is obeying the commission: is the Lord's presence evident in our midst? If not, you can be sure that there is a problem somewhere in regard to obeying the Great Commission to make disciples in all nations.

Across the centuries, the church has gained some ground through multiplication. By the end of the New Testament, there was one believer to every 360 unbelievers. Today, it is one believer to nearly seven unbelievers in the world. The church is multiplying across Africa and Asia at unbelievable rates of progress. 20,000 people per day turn to faith in Christ in Africa. In 1900, Africa was only 3% Christian. Today, it is 50% Christian. In Iran, Muslims are turning to Christ to the tune of 500 per month. These are young people since 70% of the population of Iran is under 30 years of age. The Jesus film has been translated into almost 1,000 languages and is credited for more than 200,000,000 salvations. In 1960, Christians were not allowed to live in Nepal. Today, there is a church in each of its 75 districts throughout the country with a population of some 500,000 Christians. Wonderful things are being done across the globe through God's people, whether they are individual Christians, churches, or other Christian organizations and ministries.

While this seems like a great advance, and it is, there is still much work to be done. Billions of people on earth live and die without ever hearing the name of Jesus and his good news of salvation from sin. About half of the world's people groups are considered to be unreached with the gospel. Thousands and thousands of villages have not a single congregation of believers ministering among them. Hundreds of languages are awaiting the translation of the Bible. Wycliffe translators report that there are about 7,000 languages in use in the world today. Only 500 of them have a complete Bible translation. While these conditions seem to be far away from us, there are also those people within our reach who have never heard a clear presentation of the gospel and who have never been invited to go to church. Jesus talked about the insanity of having the light of the world within us and yet hiding it, as it were, a candle under a basket, rather than on a lampstand so it can give light to the whole house.

God gave the church the command to multiply. This command is just as binding upon Christians today as it was upon those first Christians in the New Testament. We must ask ourselves the questions: "Am I multiplying disciples of Christ? Is my church seeking to multiply other congregations of believers? Am I asking God to use me to make a personal response to at least one area of need in the task of evangelizing the world's people? Have I surrendered my life to Christ that he might use me as he wants?" We live in a time of great need. According to the Bible, we live in the last days. We do not know how much time we may have to work for the Lord. Soon, he will return and we will have to account to him of how we obeyed his command to multiply. I hope you are with me in that I want to do all I can to be obedient to him, and to help forward obedience to the faith in the Lord Jesus Christ among all the nations.

**THE CHURCH MULTIPLIED**
**BLOCK 5 - THEME 3 - LESSON 3 (155 OF 216)**
**LESSON OUTLINE**

**I THE MULTIPLICATION OF CHRISTIANS**
- A. Addition
- B. Multiplication

**II THE MULTIPLICATION OF CHURCHES**
- A. In the book of Acts
- B. In the world today
- C. More work needed today
  1. Evangelism
  2. Disciple-making
  3. Bible translation

**SCRIPTURES TO BROADEN YOUR UNDERSTANDING**

1. The multiplication of disciples
   Acts 6:1

2. We have all we need to make disciples
   2 Timothy 1:9-10

**LINES OF THEOLOGICAL CONNECTION**

1. THE DOCTRINE OF THE CHURCH
   The great commission

2. CHRISTOLOGY
   Christ promised to be with us as we fulfill his commission

**THE CHURCH MULTIPLIED**
**BLOCK 5 - THEME 3 - LESSON 3 (155 OF 216)**
**QUESTIONS**

1. Name the two numbers in which a church should be interested.

2. In what mission is every Christian to be engaged?

3. List two reasons why a Christian does not multiply.

4. On what condition did Jesus promise to be with us today?

5. What do you think about the growth of the church in other countries today?

6. What do you think about the work yet to be done in sharing the gospel and translating the Bible into other languages?

7. What are you personally doing to multiply disciples of Christ?

8. Research Wycliffe Bible Translators on the internet. Take a look at all the available jobs and careers through this wonderful ministry. Do you see one that appeals to you?

# 12. THE CHURCH PERSECUTED

## THEME: THE CHURCH IN THE BIBLE

BLOCK 5 - THEME 3 - LESSON 4

**LESSON AIM:** Show that Christians should expect persecution in one degree or another.

**SCRIPTURE:** (Matthew 5:10-12)

*10 Blessed are they which are persecuted for righteousness' sake: for theirs is the kingdom of heaven. 11 Blessed are ye, when men shall revile you, and persecute you, and shall say all manner of evil against you falsely, for my sake. 12 Rejoice, and be exceeding glad: for great is your reward in heaven: for so persecuted they the prophets which were before you.*

There is a struggle between two forces in the world. The most common identification of these two forces is good and evil. When we begin to examine these forces, we learn that there are personalities behind them. The Bible reveals that the persons behind these forces of good and evil are God and Satan. John referred to them as the Spirit of God and the spirit of antichrist.

We often say that man is caught in the middle of the struggle between these two forces but this is not an altogether true statement. A more accurate statement is that man is on one side or the other in this epic struggle between good and evil, God and Satan. When we are born into the world, we are on the side of Satan because of The Fall. Through the grace of God in salvation in Christ Jesus, we can move over on the side of God.

To be on the side of God in the struggle between good and evil demands that we become active participants in the fight. To be on God's side and to expect that we do not have to join in the fight is unrealistic. If we take this stance, we will experience pressure from God to join in the struggle. If we refuse to join in the struggle, God may use other ways to deal with our rebellion. On the other hand, since we are on the opposing side in the conflict, we should expect to experience opposition from the adversary. There are many weapons the enemy has to use against us, but often times, his opposition comes in the form of persecution.

In the spiritual sense, the world is a battlefield and the Christian has been dropped behind enemy lines. Every step we take as a Christian toward the cause and mission of Christ is an encroachment of enemy held territory. The enemy is not going to take this encroachment lightly. To lose an inch, to him, is a push toward his inevitable destruction which God promised immediately after Satan caused man to fall into sin. The enemy holds tightly to his position in the world and will not give it up freely or easily. In an effort to keep Christians from becoming too bold in their attempts to take his territory, the adversary uses the weapon of persecution to try to keep Christians from using the power they have in God. Sometimes, it works as Satan would like for it to work. Sometimes, God turns it around and uses it for good.

Persecution, as it relates to Christianity, is any form of hostility from the world in response to a person's association with Jesus Christ. Persecution should not come as a surprise to us. Jesus warned us to expect it. He even identified some places where it might come from. Our focal passage for this lesson gives us three points to consider about the persecution of Christians.

First, Jesus said that congratulations are in order for those who are persecuted for righteousness sake. To be blessed is more than simply being fortunate enough to receive something, or to be happy because of that receipt. To be blessed also carried with it some understanding that the one who was blessed was to receive some congratulations from the one who was doing the blessing. So Jesus, to some degree, is saying that God's congratulations go to those Christians who suffer persecution for his name's sake. When God allows the persecution, he always has a purpose for it which has something to do with his global cause. When we draw the fire of the enemy because of our union with Christ and because of our service and devotion to him, God offers us his congratulations for our stand with him in the fight against Satan and evil.

Jesus went on to say that there are cruelties associated with persecution. He mentioned persecution coming in the form of insults and false accusations. A reading of the Bible also plainly reveals much more severe forms of persecution. Church history concurs with the testimony of Scripture concerning various forms and degrees of persecution. The church and Christians have experienced almost every imaginable thing from discrimination, to insults, slavery, isolation, torture, severe punishment, rape, and death. The twentieth century saw more persecution of Christians than all the other centuries together in the history of the church. Today, Christians experience many acts of violence against them. Many of their worship centers are destroyed each year. And, many people die each year for their faith in Jesus Christ. We have recently seen the persecution of Christians in the Middle East by the radical Muslim group, ISIS, and their beheadings broadcast across all our news and social media. We see that Christians are still dying for their faith in Christ, now in numbers more than ever.

As a final note from out text, Jesus spoke of the company we have in persecution. He reminded us that his prophets had been treated this way, too. Hebrews 11 tells us of many others who loved not their lives unto the death that joined the company of the persecuted. Jesus himself received such treatment. He warned that if they treated him in this way, we should expect no less when we align ourselves with him. Persecution is the lot of the believer. But, think of the giants of the faith in whose company we stand when persecution comes our way. The Bible declares that the world was not worthy of such heroes.

As a Christian, it is likely that you will face some form of persecution in your life time. As we have shown, this persecution may come in many forms, from mild to severe. Prepare yourself for it before it comes. Determine that you will endure it for the testimony of Jesus Christ. Keep your eyes on Christ as he will be with you during those times.

Also, remember those who are suffering severe persecution around the world. Many of our brothers and sisters in Christ are facing much more difficult situations than are we. Pray for them. Inform yourself about the persecution of Christians around the world. If God leads you, get involved in a ministry that serves the persecuted church. You can find several of them by internet search. Hebrews 13:3 tells us to remember those who are in bonds as if we were in bonds with them. And to remember those who suffer as if we were with them in their suffering. In this way, the body of Christ shows its unity and ministers to itself in times of suffering.

If you are called upon to suffer persecution, remember that God's congratulations go to those who suffer persecution. You may experience persecution in various forms, from mild to severe. Remember that you are in good company as you suffer. And, remember what Jesus suffered for us that we might be called the children of God.

**THE CHURCH PERSECUTED**
**BLOCK 5 - THEME 3 - LESSON 4 (156 OF 216)**
**LESSON OUTLINE**

**I CONGRATULATIONS TO THE PERSECUTED**
- A. "Blessed" = congratulations
- B. Persecution comes when we stand for Christ and his cause

**II CRUELTIES ASSOCIATED WITH PERSECUTION**
- A. From mild
- B. To severe

**III THE COMPANY OF THE PERSECUTED**
- A. The Old Testament prophets
- B. Other Christians
- C. Jesus

**SCRIPTURES TO BROADEN YOUR UNDERSTANDING**

1. Jesus was persecuted
   John 5:16
   John 15:20

2. The church persecuted
   Acts 8:1
   Acts 13:50
   2 Timothy 3:12

3. Endure sufferings
   2 Timothy 2:3

4. 2 Spirits in the world
   1 John 4:1-4

5. Satan's methods
   Ephesians 6:11
   2 Corinthians 2:11

**LINES OF THEOLOGICAL CONNECTION**

1. CHRISTOLOGY
   The sufferings of Christ

2. THE DOCTRINE OF THE CHURCH
   The persecution of believers

3. ANTHROPOLOGY
   Endure suffering
   Support the persecuted

**THE CHURCH PERSECUTED**
**BLOCK 5 - THEME 3 - LESSON 4 (156 OF 216)**
**QUESTIONS**

1. What is persecution?

2. What are some forms persecution may take?

3. How does church persecution in the 20th century compare to that of other centuries?

4. Have you ever been persecuted for your belief in the Lord Jesus Christ?

5. Go to www.opendoorsusa.org and learn about the present day persecution of believers around the world. Is God calling you to work in this area of ministry?

## 13. THE FIRST 500 YEARS

## THEME: A BRIEF CHURCH HISTORY

BLOCK 5 - THEME 4 - LESSON 1

**LESSON AIM:** Give a brief history of the church's first 500 years.

**SCRIPTURE:** (Matthew 16:18)

*"I will build my church; and the gates of hell shall not prevail against it."*
*Jesus.*

The birth of the church is directly connected to God's mission in the world. All the way back in Genesis 3:15, we learned that since man's fall into sin, God has been on a mission to rescue and restore fallen man from sin and condemnation. God promised to send a deliverer who would both save the lost and destroy the works of the devil in the process. This deliverer is Jesus Christ and the work he did to accomplish both of these objectives was to die on the cross as a redemptive sacrifice and to rise again from the dead.

As a part of his plan, God chose a man named Abram through whom he would bring the Messiah into the world. From Abram, God made a nation of people called the Hebrews. The Hebrews were commissioned to take the news of the Savior to all peoples of the earth. Being a hard-hearted and rebellious people, the Hebrews refused to accept the Messiah and his evangelistic purpose for them. God took this privilege from the Jews and gave it to another people. He raised up another group from all the nations to whom he would transfer the responsibility of this work. This group is called the church.

The church has existed for just over 2,000 years. Her beginnings are found in the New Testament book of Acts and in the letters of the apostles. Her history is one of battle, blood and bruises. The world has tried to destroy her time and again, but Jesus has promised that nothing would prevail against the church that he has built.

The New Testament covers a large portion of the church's first century of existence and ministry. From the days of Christ himself, to the ministry of the last apostle, the church begins to stand on wobbling knees and take her place in the world. Much of her early history sails through the blood of Christians who stood for Christ and his cause and were martyred for their faith. The apostles themselves gave their lives to advance God's purpose through his church. Only John died a natural death. All the others, as far as we know were martyred, six of them by crucifixion. Among their sufferings were beatings, torturing, burning, spearing, flaying, and beheading. They paid with their lives for being a member of the Lord's church. In spite of the bloodletting, by the end of the first century, the church had spread all across Asia Minor and into northern Africa.

The next hundred years after the apostles saw the continuance of the church through the apologists. These people were some of the disciples of the apostles. They too, took up the pen and the Scriptures to preach the gospel to the world. Like the apostles before them, many of them also died for their faith in Christ. During this time, the books of the New Testament already written, the New Testament began to formulate into its canonical form. The church struggled from problems both within itself and without. Within, the church battled heresies which sought to infiltrate the ranks of believers. Without, political and social persecution continued to hound Christians as they tried to live out their faith in the daily life. Until about 250 A.D., the persecution was localized and sporadic. Afterwards, persecution came more directly from the Roman government as Christianity was considered to be an enemy of the state. Christians who refused to worship the Roman emperor were killed. Others who insisted upon remaining loyal to Christ were imprisoned, tortured, worked to death, or killed for sport.

The emperor, Constantine, saw the Christians in a different light. He felt they could be useful in helping to save the declining empire. He issued an edict bringing an end to the persecutions for a time. Christians received some favor from Rome as Christianity eventually became the official religion of the state. It was at this time that Satan landed one of his first strategic responses to the church, which I remind you, had been kept a secret from the beginning. His blow to the church was to exploit the divisions within the church between clergy and laity and reverse their God-given priorities. What this has done was to keep the word of God from the people while at the same time making the clergy responsible for all of the work of the ministry. This was an ingenious move which the church still struggles against today.

As the church grew and struggled across the empire, more apologists arose, writing, speaking and affirming the teachings of Christianity. Councils were assembled, confirming the canon of the Scriptures, and speaking against heresies against the faith. At the same time, the global landscape was in a state of flux as peoples moved, fought and conquered other peoples and their empires. Rome was not immune from the advance of this movement and eventually fell to invasion in 410 A.D.. Other developments in North Africa would pave the way for the rise and advance of Islam in the near future.

By the end of the fourth century, the church was on its way toward carrying out the mission Jesus had given to it. From its beginning, it has always been plagued by the tendency to institutionalize, the rise of major religious opposition from without, from obvious satanic warfare, and by the fearful and apathetic hearts of many believers within. It is a wonder that the church has survived at all in light of these difficulties. However, Jesus is the head of the church, and he did say that even the gates of hell would never prevail against the church. Through the centuries, God has preserved his church and empowered it to carry out his purpose in spite of itself and the obstacles it encounters. History bears testimony of the faithfulness of the Lord Jesus to keep his promise, giving way for the church to take his story to the nations. Our prayer should be that the people of God would respond with the same kind of dedication and devotion to the Lord and his purpose as the Lord has to the church.

**THE FIRST 500 YEARS**
**BLOCK 5 - THEME 4 - LESSON 1 (157 OF 216)**
**LESSON OUTLINE**

**I GOD PROMISED TO SEND A DELIVERER**

A. The Hebrews were commissioned to evangelize the nations
B. When Israel refused her role, the church was born and commissioned

**II THE CHURCH'S FIRST 500 YEARS**

A. 1st Century - The age of the apostles
B. 2nd Century - The apologists
C. 3rd Century - Persecution continues - the church grows
D. 4th Century - Christianity becomes the state religion of Rome
E. 5th Century - Rome falls

**SCRIPTURES TO BROADEN YOUR UNDERSTANDING**

1. The church in the first century
   The entire New Testament
   Acts, in particular

**LINES OF THEOLOGICAL CONNECTION**

1. ECCLESIOLOGY
   The apostles
   The Christian apologists
   The mysteries of Israel and the church

2. CHRISTOLOGY
   The gospel
   Redemption
3. THE DOCTRINE OF GOD
   God's global purpose

4. ESCHATOLOGY
   Finishing the evangelization of the world

**LESSON GLOSSARY**

1. Martyr
   One who dies rather than renounce his faith

**THE FIRST 500 YEARS**
**BLOCK 5 - THEME 4 - LESSON 1 (157 OF 216)**
**QUESTIONS**

1. In the beginning of the church, people announced their belief in Christ at the risk of their life. Has being a believer cost you anything today?

2. Jesus said we would be his witnesses. The word “witness” comes from the Greek word for a martyr. What do you think this says about the Christian life?

3. The early church paid a great price so the church could fulfill her assignment. How are Christians today squandering this investment of the early church?

4. What investment are you making in the Lord’s church today?

5. More Christians were martyred in the 20th century than in all the other centuries combined. We have seen many Christians martyred recently by ISIS. What is your reaction when you see this happening to fellow Christians in other parts of the world?

6. The work done by the apostles and the apologists of the early church is invaluable to us today. Thank God for the lives which were given so we could hear the gospel and be saved. Thank God for the writings of these men that help us know God through the Scriptures in our time.

# 14. SCHISM

## THEME: A BRIEF CHURCH HISTORY

BLOCK 5 - THEME 4 - LESSON 2

**LESSON AIM:** Give a brief history of the church from the end of the Roman Empire to the schism. (Approximately 500 AD to 1000 AD)

God made a promise in the third chapter of Genesis and verse fifteen. Since Satan had caused the fall of man into sin and condemnation, God promised that he would send a deliverer to destroy the works of Satan and provide the way of reconciliation for the fallen. Jesus Christ was this deliverer and he accomplished these two assignments by his work on the cross. His people, Israel, refused to recognize and receive him as their Messiah, refused his kingdom, and refused the assignment he intended for them which was to take the message of redemption through Christ to all peoples of the earth. In response to Israel's rejection, God raised up the church through which he would continue his work of evangelization.

The church began its work in the book of Acts. In spite of great difficulty and persecution the church was off to a great start toward fulfilling its assignment. By the time of the end of the Roman Empire, the visible church in the world had waned from its initial fervor and had become more of a religious institution. When the Empire fell, the world was left with a religious organization, far from the apostolic design, which influenced the world of the times, and continues its influence throughout the world today.

During these years of the middle ages, the catholic church faced struggles, both within and outside of the church. Within the church, the struggle was manifested in the occurrences of the everyday life of their times. Socially, feudalism was the order of the day. Overlords and vassals contracted with each other for the use of lands through the favors they exchanged with each other. Seeing a way to enrich itself, the church threw into the mix, blurring the lines between the society and the church. Spiritually, monasticism was rising to be the most prevalent means of religious encounter. Monastic isolation, however, was not the best means for the church to be the salt and light Jesus wanted it to be.

The problems presented by the social and spiritual orders of the day essentially came down to one question: Who is going to control, or govern over the people and their problems? On the one hand, the church assumed itself to be the appropriate authority. On the other hand, there was the emperor. Over the years, at various times, each one would take its turn at the top of the hill. Their struggle to be the final authority would continue for centuries.

While the church was struggling to establish, expand, and maintain its hold in the places already gained, the outside world presented other problems of its own. Heretical churches of various sorts had sprung up throughout the world of the day; Nestorians, Donatists, Marcionites, Montanists, and Gnostics to name a few. Taking a facet of the truth and promoting an interpretation of that facet against the prevailing church doctrine was the basis of fostering a "new" church. Also, emerging and sweeping throughout the world was Islam. Within one hundred years of its origin in 622, Islam had already spread to India, Northern Africa, and Spain. With so many problems to address, changes taking place, rivals on the scene, and misguided ambitions, the church experienced a division which was a long time coming, and continues into the present time.

The church split into two churches in 1054, each claiming to be catholic, or universal. The Orthodox Church prevailed in the East and continues today with some 300 million followers. From its beginning, it claimed to be the church handed down by the apostles themselves. Having a great appreciation for the past and for the Bible, this reverence has always been an attraction. Historically, the Orthodox Church has been the point man for the church on the front of persecution. No other part of the church has paid so much in martyr's blood as has the Orthodox Church at the hands of Communists, Mongols, and Muslims across the years. However, in spite of its reverence for the Word of God and willingness to die for it, the Orthodox Church has suffered from a poor vision for the lost of the world. With little vision for missions, the church suffers from decline today.

In the West, the Roman Catholic Church ruled supreme. After the schism into eastern and western churches, the western church stepped up its agenda to assert its authority, influence, and control over all it possibly could. Wielding the weapons of persecution, excommunication, and execution, the church could advance it's cause. As stated earlier, the church continually exerted itself in spiritual affairs certainly, but also in social affairs. The struggle continued for which entity would be the authority, the church or the emperor. With its hands in the money pot, and with so many of the church's leadership participating in the feudal system, a showdown emerged between Pope Gregory VII and Henry IV, and for a time, the papacy gained the upper hand over the authority of the emperor.

The condition of the unbridled exertion of the church into any and every area paved the way for both the temporal wealth and the spiritual bankruptcy of the Roman Catholic Church. For a time, the church seemed to free-wheel, taking advantage of its grasp of everything from the throne to the peasant. Having the Scriptures quarantined from the common people, the church could easily write and promote its own agenda of greed and control. And this it did to perfection.

Although the church appeared to be unstoppable, there was already a dissention brewing below the surface. It is amazing to see that the machine of the church which had such an oppressive grasp around the throats of the people of the world could be opposed and changed by only a small handful of individuals. Here and there, God was working in the hearts of men and women to bring about a change. Hundreds of years more of this decline and corruption were on the way, but eventually this change would come.

In the midst of a visible but corrupt church in the world, The Lord was still at work growing, and preserving his true church. Soon the time would come when his chosen champions of reform would rise up and be the force that would move the true church in another direction.

**SCHISM**
**BLOCK 5 - THEME 4 - LESSON 2 (158 OF 216)**
**LESSON OUTLINE**

**I STRUGGLES**
- A. Within the Church
  - 1. The Struggles
    - a. Social - Feudalism
    - b. Spiritual - Monasticism
  - 2. Control of the struggles
    - a. The church?
    - b. The Emperor?
- B. Outside the Church
  - 1. Heretics
  - 2. Islam

**II SCHISM**
- A. Divisions of the Church
  - 1. Roman Catholics in the West
  - 2. Eastern Orthodox in the East
- B. Papal authority in the West

**SCRIPTURES TO BROADEN YOUR UNDERSTANDING**

1. The parable of the wheat and the tares
   Matthew 13:24-30

**LINES OF THEOLOGICAL CONNECTION**

1. ECCLESIOLOGY
   The history of the church
   The Roman Catholic Church
   The Eastern Orthodox Church
   The Reformation

**LESSON GLOSSARY**

1. Schism
   A formal division within a religious body.

2. Catholic
   Universal.

3. Excommunication
   To cut off officially from the rites of the church

**SCHISM**
**BLOCK 5 - THEME 4 - LESSON 2 (158 OF 216)**
**QUESTIONS**

1. Within 500 years of the death and resurrection of Christ, the true church became overshadowed by the church left to the world by the fall of the Roman Empire. What was an easy clue to know the difference between the two?

2. The church of the state was eventually divided into two churches which continue today. What are they?

3. In what year did the schism officially take place?

4. Both the eastern and western churches claimed to be the catholic church. What does catholic mean?

5. What were three weapons mentioned in the lesson which were used by the Roman Catholic church to exert its influence and authority in the world?

6. The Roman Catholic Church had much power and influence, was growing wealthy, but was declining spiritually. What term was used in the lesson to describe the church's spiritual condition?

7. What tools do we have today to help us discern the difference between the true church of the Lord Jesus Christ and an imposter?

# 15. REFORMATION

## THEME: A BRIEF CHURCH HISTORY

BLOCK 5 - THEME 4 - LESSON 3

**LESSON AIM:** Give a brief history of the church from the schism to the reformation. (Approximately 1000 AD to 1500 AD)

**SCRIPTURE:** (Romans 1:17)

*"For therein is the righteousness of God revealed from faith to faith: as it is written, The just shall live by faith."*

The Roman Catholic Church in the west was a church with two natures. On the social and political fronts, the church was powerful and wealthy. The combination of these two things gave the church a boldness to continue its steamroller advance over everything and everybody. The spiritual nature of the church, however, was just the opposite. Corruption, greed, and cruelty were the standard operating procedures of the day. It is not too much to say that the church was nearly spiritually bankrupt.

While the church was in very bad spiritual condition, at the same time the monastic movement was at its height. Some of the only bright spots for the Roman Catholic Church during this time were to be found among the monks of the Franciscan order. They were humble Christ-followers of the church but inspired others to break free from the church. Another order of monks, the Dominicans, were the hound dogs of the church against heresy and schism. They were the kind of people the church needed for its Holy Office of Inquisition to combat heresy. The church was in desperate need of reform and change.

Out of the church at this time came the Crusades. The goals of the crusades were two-fold. First, the church wanted to grant access to the sites of the holy land which were under Muslim control. Second, the pope, Urban II, hoped to reunite the eastern and western churches under his authority. Overall, the crusades largely failed to accomplish either goal. They did, however, open trade routes and encouraged commerce which became a river of wealth into the Roman Catholic Church. Another result of the crusades was the animosity of the Muslims toward Christians which still hinders relations between them in the world today.

One of the digressions of the church at this time was the sale of church offices. Policies related to this practice came back to bite them, contributing to more decline and division. Pope Boniface VIII sought to establish papal authority universally and forbade the taxation of the clergy. King Philip IV of France stood against him, eventually leading to the election of a Frenchman as pope. For a period of some seventy years, the papacy was seated in France instead of Rome. This period was called by the Italians, The Babylonian Captivity.

One of the consequences of the Babylonian captivity was the Great Schism, not to be confused with the schism of the church into east and west churches. The papacy moved back to Rome and another man was elected as pope, Urban VI. Turning out to be a poor choice, he was rejected and replaced by Clement VII in France. Unfortunately, Urban refused to give up his role and continued to go about his work. Now the church had two popes, and before it was over, three. Eventually all three popes were deposed and replaced by Martin V at the Council of Constance. This action brought an end to the Great Schism in 1417.

Although the Great Schism was ended, the church and the papacy were left in a weakened condition. The political weakness of the church continued to be taken advantage of by empires and rulers which had recently come into being and power. Spiritually, the church had never been any farther from the truth and from holiness. Socially, they were losing their grip as more and more people became wise to the reality of it all.

Leading the way among the pre-reformers of the church were the likes of John Wyclif and John Huss. They challenged the interpretations of the church concerning a number of its teachings. They worked to get the Scriptures in the hands of the common man, teaching them to understand God's Word for themselves. Both men suffered various forms of persecution from the church, Huss being burned alive at the stake.

The church, spiritually bankrupt and having lost its way, suffered from a number of factors. The leaders themselves lived lives of greed and immorality. Many doctrines taught by the church went directly against the teaching of the Word of God. The common man had been deprived of the Scriptures, leaving the door open for the church to use them against the people rather than for them. Secular writings and documents which exposed the falsehoods of the Roman Catholic Church were also out of the reach of the everyday person. Not willing to stand by and lose what it had gained over the centuries, ill-gotten as it was, the church continued to respond with more persecution. Finally, with the church at or certainly near the bottom of the barrel, the time of reformation had come.

Another despicable practice of the Roman Catholic Church was the sale of indulgences. The church was selling forgiveness to people who hoped to get their loved ones out of purgatory and earn some credit against their own sins as well. Money was made for the church in this way, hand over fist, so much so that the likes of St. Peter's Basilica could be funded while padding the pockets of church officials at the same time. This practice drew priest and professor, Martin Luther, out of the shadows, giving a face to the Protestant Reformation. He wrote and posted a document known as The Ninety-Five Theses, a list of grievances against the church, to the church doors in Wittenberg, Germany. He went on to call out other corruptions within the church and to stand for the authority of the Scriptures. His boldness inspired others to rise up for reform as well. Before it was over, Luther had led a movement that shook up the Roman Catholic Church and opened the door for the development of the Protestant Church into the present time.

From the days of the church just after apostolic times, the church divided itself time and time again. The schism of 1054 left us with the Eastern Orthodox Church and the Roman Catholic Church. The reformation brought on a new wave of protestant churches. Our next lesson will follow this vane into the 20th century.

**REFORMATION**
**BLOCK 5 - THEME 4 - LESSON 3 (159 OF 216)**
**LESSON OUTLINE**

**I PRE-REFORMATION**
- A. The Crusades
- B. The Babylonian Captivity
- C. The Great Schism
- D. Further spiritual decline of the church
- E. The pre-reformers

**II THE REFORMATION**
- A. A summary of the problems
- B. Reformation
  - 1. Magisterial
  - 2. Radical

**LINES OF THEOLOGICAL CONNECTION**

1. ECCLESIOLOGY
   The reformation
   The reformers
   The Roman Catholic Church

**REFORMATION**
**BLOCK 5 - THEME 4 - LESSON 3 (159 OF 216)**
**QUESTIONS**

1. From this lesson, what two events from church history still influence the world in which we live in today?

2. Who is the most well-known reformer of the reformation?

3. What practice of the church tipped the scales for Martin Luther?

4. What bold move did Martin Luther make to mark the beginning of the reformation?

5. Although it was not the only place where reform had started to take place, where did Martin Luther take his stand against the church?

6. Have you ever felt the need to take a stand for God in the midst of a group which was against him? Explain.

7. Do you think you could take a stand for God if it meant losing your life?

8. Read Foxes Book of Martyrs about those who died for their faith in Christ.

# 16. BEYOND THE REFORMATION

## THEME: A BRIEF CHURCH HISTORY

BLOCK 5 - THEME 4 - LESSON 4

**LESSON AIM:** Give a brief history of the church from the reformation to the present. (Approximately 1500 AD to 2015)

**SCRIPTURE:** (Ephesians 3:20-21)

*Now unto him that is able to do exceeding abundantly above all that we ask or think, according to the power that worketh in us, unto him be glory in the church by Christ Jesus throughout all ages, world without end. Amen.*

The church was born in the first century and flourished to the extent of the Roman Empire. When the empire fell, the world was left with the church of the state. The church of the state divided itself into the church of the East and the church of the West. The church in the West became so corrupt it had to be reformed. The reformation paved the way for the sweeping changes in the church the world has seen during the last 500 years. This lesson considers three factors which have contributed to these changes.

The last 500 years have been marked by an ever shrinking world. Explorations around the globe opened doors to new places and opportunities to escape persecutions with the possibility of a fresh start. As people moved into new worlds and flourished into advancing societies, they began to take their advances into other worlds with them. As nations became powerful and industrialized, they moved into new places where they could find more resources needed to make their products and a buyer base to which to sell them. The exchange was not always fair, the advantage going more to the industrialized nation. As nations advanced through industry, many times the church went along with them into these new places. Unfortunately, the church was often connected to the negative results of industrial advance and was, many times, rejected for this reason. Wars escalating to the global scale also brought peoples of different cultures into contact with each other, contributing to the shrinking of the world.

Technological advances in many areas have also played a part in shrinking the world. Around the time of the reformation came the printing press, making it possible to put the new translations of the Bible into the hands of more and more common people. More advances across the years in communications, including the telegraph, the telephone, the computer and the digital age continue to work to put people in touch with the press of a button or by the swipe of a finger. Advancing travel modes have made it possible to be almost anywhere on the planet in a short amount of time. Trips that once took months by ship have been reduced to mere days and hours. The shrinking world has been a huge factor in the changes in the church since the reformation.

The reformation also opened the door to much division in the church of recent centuries. Divisions took place in the church in the East and in the West. The Orthodox Church divided into several parts including Russian, Greek, and Serbian Orthodox Churches. In the West, the Roman Catholic Church continued to divide again to east and west subdivisions, as well as the emergence of the Church of England and its Anglican and Protestant manifestations.

Protestantism continues to divide into more and more denominations today. The divisions among Protestants trace back to the reformation as people had the Word of God in their own hands for the first time. Disagreements over how to interpret the Scriptures have led to many of the divisions among us. Two things were designed to produce unity in the church: doctrine and purpose. Each of these unity producers have come under attack, shown by the number of divisions among us. If we cannot agree on how the Scripture is to be understood, we cannot agree on what we are to do as the church in the world.

Fulfilling our mission has been replaced by promoting our piece of the division within the church. Gordon-Conwell Theological Seminary says that in 2012, there were some 43,000 denominations in Christianity. By 2025, there are estimated to be in the neighborhood of 55,000. Every day, more than two new denominations come into being as the church continues to be divided. There are more Christian denominations than there are verses in the Bible. The Word of God should unite us, not divide us. We are approaching a time when there are almost two denominations for every verse in the Bible. At some point, we might need to recognize the absurdity of all this division.

A final factor contributing to the changes in the church in the last 500 years is the missionary movement. In spite of the division within the church, much advancement has been made in reaching the people of the world with the gospel. This is proof of the words of Jesus when he said the gates of hell would not prevail against the church. Though the enemy seeks to divide the church, it is still taking the gospel to the nations.

The missionary advance of the church has developed in three stages. The first stage was the advance into the coastal areas of the world (1800 to 1910). This stage in missionary movement rode on the heels of the Great Awakening which sparked the American Revolution. Following the Revolution, a lull in enthusiasm for the work of the Lord was motivated by a Second Great Awakening, helping to move Christians into mission fields beyond the home front. British missionary William Carey, known as the father of modern missions, stood as an example during this period as he advanced missionary work in India.

A second stage of missionary movement took missions deeper into the interior of the countries being penetrated with the gospel. This period of time in the modern church, while seeing many great missionary works done for the Lord, may be one of the reasons for the decline of the church today. During this period (1865 to 1980) churches wrestled with the question of being the church versus doing church. With the rise of parachurch organizations such as the great China Inland Mission founded by Hudson Taylor, and other ministries like it, many churches opted for doing church while they gave their offering to others to do their missionary work for them. This is by no means an attack on Taylor's great work but an indictment against the church for allowing the enemy to use missions against it. While the church gave money to others to do mission work, it rode the crest of the wave of the Good Ol' Days until all the energy had gone out of the wave. In those days, the church paid more attention to itself than to discipling others to continue its ministry beyond the current time. Now, here we are today with many churches dead or dying, struggling to continue their ministry. The great lesson in this is to find the balance between being the church and in doing church. We have to do each of them.

Since the mid 1930's, the church has ventured into another stage of the missionary movement; missions and ministry among the people groups of the world (1935 to present). Seeing the need to distinguish between the nations of the world and the unique ways each one of them have to be reached with the gospel, the church has sought to plant the church among people groups where it has never been planted before. People groups have been identified and categorized as either reached with the gospel or unreached. Missionary work continues or not today based on these categories.

When the gospel is taken to a new people group, the pattern is very similar on the surface. Since each group is different on a cultural level, the specifics vary from one group to another group. Generally speaking, the pattern is as follows. The gospel enters the group by any number of possible ways. When the gospel is shared, by the power of the Holy Spirit, regeneration takes place in the people and the gospel begins to advance among the people group. Once this advance begins, the adversary sets opposition in the path of the gospel advance. Opposition may take many forms from mild to severe, including death to the missionary evangelist. Then, with a new foothold among another people group, the church settles in to endure the opposition, to grow and continue to advance among this people group and beyond to others. When the missionaries have established the church and have discipled them to reproduce, they can move to a new frontier and begin the process all over again with another people group.

The church has had a long history of struggle and opposition. Like the parable of the wheat and the tares, the true church has had to do its work while an imposter church rivals it in the world. Christ, the head of the church, knows the difference between the two. His Word tells us how to know the difference as well. The true church is the body of Christ in the world assigned to take the gospel into the final frontiers of the gospel advance. When the church is complete, Jesus will come for it so he can turn to Israel and bring them into the blessing he wants them to enjoy. Until then, we must continue to do the work, following Christ into all places where he opens the door for his people to witness of himself.

**BEYOND THE REFORMATION**
**BLOCK 5 - THEME 4 - LESSON 4 (160 OF 216)**
**LESSON OUTLINE**

**I A SHRINKING WORLD**

A. Exploration
B. Industrialization
C. World Wars
D. Technological advances

**II A DIVIDING CHURCH**
- A. The Eastern Orthodox Church
- B. The Roman Catholic Church
- C. Protestantism

**III THE MISSIONARY MOVEMENT**
- A. Development
  - 1. Coastal regions
  - 2. Inland regions
  - 3. People groups
- B. The pattern of the gospel
  - 1. Entrance
  - 2. Advancement
  - 3. Opposition
  - 4. Endurance

**LINES OF THEOLOGICAL CONNECTION**

1. ECCLESIOLOGY
   The history of the church after the reformation

**BEYOND THE REFORMATION**
**BLOCK 5 - THEME 4 - LESSON 4 (160 OF 216)**
**QUESTIONS**

1. What does the phrase mean, "the shrinking of the world"?

2. List some contributing factors to the shrinking of the world.

3. What are the three periods of missionary advance after the reformation?

4. What was the controversy in the church during the period of inland missionary advance?

5. By what was the struggle of the previous question fueled?

6. While churches gave money to others to do mission work for them, what did they do?

7. What is the focus of missionary work in our day?

8. How are you involved in the missionary effort of the church?

# 17. ORGANIZATION AND PRIORITIES

## THEME: THE LOCAL CHURCH

BLOCK 5 - THEME 5 - LESSON 1

**LESSON AIM:** The Bible gives us a basic organizational structure for the local church and sets the priorities for each part.

**SCRIPTURE:** (Acts 6:1-7)

The church is generally thought of in two ways. First, there is the universal church. This is the entire body of Christ around the world and in every generation. This includes all believers of all nations from the beginning of the church in The New Testament to the time when the church is completed. Every believer is a part of the universal church. The second way we think of the church is as the local church in our towns and communities around the world. Local churches vary in size, demographics, and how they operate and carry out the mission God has given the church.

There are three basic questions the local church should ask as it begins its work for God. They should ask, what are we to do, how should we organize ourselves in order to do what we are supposed to do, and what are the priorities within our organizational structure? The first question is answered with the great commission to make disciples in all nations. Much of this entire course is given to address this commission. This lesson will focus on the answers to the second and third questions.

Acts 6:1-7 is a text that gives us the Bible answer to these two questions. Let's first consider the basic organizational structure the Bible gives for the local church. This structure is seen in the use of the word "deacon" in the text. The English reader of the King James Bible might say that the word deacon does not appear in the text at all. In the original language, however, it appears three times in relation to the three groups which make up the organizational structure of the church.

Let's take the words in reverse order as they appear in the text. In verse four, the word appears in the word "ministry". This is a reference to the men who pastor the local church. Next, in verse two, the word appears in the word "serve" at the end of the verse. This refers to those men who serve in the office of the deacon within the local church. The third reference is in verse one in the word "ministration". This is a reference to the ministry of the largest group within the church, the remaining people who do not serve as pastors or deacons. These three groups then become the basic structure of the local church.

It is important to note the classification of the groups as well. The first two groups serve in the official capacity within the local church; pastors and deacons. These two groups are called offices in The New Testament. They are the main spiritual leadership within the local church. The third group functions in an operative capacity. That is, they are the main work force of the church. It is through these people, primarily, that God intended to carry out the mission of the great commission. The officials are to lead them, prepare them, and mobilize them to accomplish this task.

As this Bible passage gives us the basic organizational structure for the local church, it also sets the priorities for each group. Let us note these priorities. Verse four says the priority of the pastor is prayer and the ministry of the word. This means that the pastor takes on the dual role similar to the Old Testament roles of priest and prophet. Prayer suggests the priestly role as the pastor goes before God on behalf of the people. The ministry of the word suggests the prophetic role as the pastor goes before the people on behalf of God. The pastor is to get the mind and heart of God for the direction and ministry of the church. He then goes about the work of communicating that vision to the people. He teaches and equips and prepares them for their work in this ministry.

The priority of the deacon office, according to verse two and three of this passage of Scripture, is to take those people who have been equipped and mobilize them to the work of the ministry. This can be done by further organizing the people according to the predominate spiritual gifts named in Romans 12. This means that the deacons will have to know the people very well, they will have to know their spiritual gifts, and they will have to know the work that needs to be done. In this way, they can help mobilize the right people to the right tasks.

Finally, verse one tells us that the priority of the people is the daily work of the ministry. It is primarily the task of the people of the church to carry out the ministries that need to be done in order for the local church to be obedient to the great commission. This is both within the church and on the outside of the church in the community and the world. The pastor and deacons are to model the ministry, teach the people how to do it, and mobilize them to the work.

This structure and priorities are basic and logical to the success of any organization. In any business there is the central leader (pastor). He has managers (deacons) who see that his vision for accomplishing the company's goals gets carried out by the people (the congregation) who work for the company. Local churches who follow this model find the most important success.

It would be great if every local church followed this simple instruction from the Word of God. Unfortunately, the devil has turned the entire plan a complete 180 degrees and the church operates in reverse order. In many churches, the work force does little to nothing, while the role of the deacon has become to see that the pastor is held responsible to do all of the work of the ministry. These churches are dead or dying and will never be what God wants them to be until they reverse this reversal of priorities and follow the Biblical model as it is written.

When the local church acknowledges God's structure and priorities, the church can flourish, grow, and accomplish its mission of fulfilling the great commission. Conflicts can be held to a minimum, and relationships can develop in a godly environment. People will also be drawn to this kind of church. May we all do our part to see that the church follows the Bible's plans for structuring and prioritizing our ministry.

**ORGANIZATION AND PRIORITIES**
**BLOCK 5 - THEME 5 - LESSON 1 (161 OF 216)**
**LESSON OUTLINE**

Two questions for the local church:

**I HOW DOES THE BIBLE ORGANIZE THE LOCAL CHURCH?**

A. The official group
   1. Pastor - Visionary
   2. Deacons - Management and mobilization

B. The operative group
   1. The people - The work force

**II WHAT ARE THE PRIORITIES FOR EACH GROUP?**

A. Pastor
   1. Prayer - To go before God on behalf of the people
   2. Ministry of the Word - To go before the people on behalf of God

B. Deacon
   1. Manage the people
   2. Mobilize the people

C. People
   1. The daily work of the ministry

**SCRIPTURES TO BROADEN YOUR UNDERSTANDING**

1. The spiritual gifts
   Romans 12

**LINES OF THEOLOGICAL CONNECTION**

1. ECCLESIOLOGY
   Church organization
   Church autonomy
   The church's commission
   Role of the pastor
   Role of the deacon
   Role of church members

2. THE DOCTRINE OF SATAN
   Satan's strategies against the church

**ORGANIZATION AND PRIORITIES**
**BLOCK 5 - THEME 5 - LESSON 1 (161 OF 216)**
**QUESTIONS**

1. Name the two ways that we may think of the church.

2. List the three questions a local church should ask as it begins its work for God.

3. What word from Acts 6:1-7 is our clue to the organizational structure of the local church?

4. As seen in the word "deacon", how does the Bible organize the local church body?

5. What are the roles of the three groups within the church?

6. What is the devil's counterstrategy against the organization and priorities of the church?

7. What can be the results of following the Biblical pattern for church organization?

# 18. THE ORDINANCES

## THEME: THE LOCAL CHURCH

BLOCK 5 - THEME 5 - LESSON 2

**LESSON AIM:** Present and briefly explain the two ordinances of the church.

**SCRIPTURE:** (Acts 2:41-42)

*"Then they that gladly received his word were baptized: and the same day there were added unto them about three thousand souls. And they continued stedfastly in the apostles' doctrine and fellowship, and in breaking of bread, and in prayers."*

Everyone who has attended worship services in the Christian church has eventually seen a baptismal service or a service in which the Lord's Supper was observed. To an outsider, perhaps these activities seem a bit unusual. They may wonder what these things are all about, what do they mean, and why do we do them? This lesson will present a brief explanation of the two ordinances observed in the Christian church, from the Baptist point of view.

The Christian church observes two ordinances as a regular part of its worship and obedience to God. We observe these ordinances primarily for two reasons. The first reason we observe the ordinances is because Jesus commanded us to do so. Jesus was baptized, although for a different reason than we are baptized, and he commanded his followers to be baptized as well. In his great commission of Matthew's gospel, the Lord told his followers to baptize those who believe in the name of the Father, and the Son, and the Holy Ghost. Jesus also commanded his followers to observe the Lord's Supper until he returns for the church. We observe the ordinances in obedience to the Lord's commands to do so. Second, we observe these two ordinances because we see that the early church observed them. This is evident in the focal passage for this lesson. We see the early church obeying the Lord's commands to baptize and have the Lord's Supper. We conclude that the Lord commanded it, the early church obeyed the commands and set the example that we are to follow today, and until the Lord comes again.

The Baptist church refers to baptism and the Lord's Supper as ordinances. Some churches may call them sacraments. What difference does it make what they are called? The word, sacrament, conveys the idea of something mysterious, and suggests that God's grace and power are actually conveyed through the observance of the ritual. While the believer is certainly blessed through the observance of these commands, Baptists believe they are symbolic and illustrative of God's work of grace, rather than the means of how his grace is conveyed to his people. Therefore, we choose to use the word, ordinance, instead of sacrament. Ordinance conveys the idea of a symbolic occurrence rather than an actual one.

Christian baptism is rich with symbolism and meaning. It is perhaps the first act of obedience performed by the new believer in Christ. The believer, soon after the salvation experience, obeys Christ by being baptized. The idea is that this instant obedience should become the standard for how a believer in Christ walks in obedience to his commands.

Baptism is an identification. In the church, it is comparable to the rite of circumcision practiced by the Jews in the Old Testament. Also, in the same way that a wedding band identifies a person as being married, baptism identifies the observer as a follower of the Lord Jesus Christ. Baptism is also the means by which a believer identifies with a local congregation of believers. Typically, when a person is baptized in a particular church, he becomes a member of that local church.

By the use of the symbol, baptism is an illustration of at least two important realities. Baptism illustrates the death burial and resurrection of the Lord Jesus Christ. During the actual baptism, when the person is laid back into the water, the Lord's death is illustrated. That brief second or two when the person is under the water symbolizes Christ in the grave. And, of course when the person is raised out of the water, we see a living illustration of the Lord's resurrection from the dead. Each time we witness the baptism of a believer, God is reminding us of the Lord's death and resurrection on our behalf and that he is still alive today. Baptism also illustrates that the person being baptized has experienced death to the old sinful man, and through his belief in Christ, has been raised to walk a new life in Christ.

From the meaning of the word, baptize, Baptists believe in baptism by immersion. We believe the person being baptized should be completely submerged in the water. Submerging is not only true to the meaning of the word, but also illustrates the believer's total involvement in the work of the Lord as his follower. When the believer emerges from the water, he is then to get involved in the work God is doing in the world.

The Lord's Supper is just as full of meaning and significance as is baptism. A key passage on the Lord's Supper is 1 Corinthians 11:20-34. This passage gives us several key points in the observance of the Lord's Supper. First, when we observe the Lord's Supper, we are to remember the person and the work of Christ. We look back to his life on earth as the sinless Son of God, and we remember that he gave himself as a sacrifice for us on the cross, paying the penalty for our sins.

As we remember the Lord's death, we also proclaim it to those who may be observing us as we observe it. It becomes a way of preaching the gospel as we see the body of Christ and the blood of Christ depicted in the elements of the bread and the juice. We see that his body was broken for us and his blood was shed for us and that we must receive it if we are going to be delivered from condemnation.

The Lord's Supper looks forward to the return of Christ for his church. Jesus said by observing this memorial meal, we are showing the Lord's death until he comes. As we participate in the Lord's Supper, we can be reminded of the Lord's promise to return for his church and take us to where he is. The church is not looking for the wrath of God that is coming upon this world. We have been delivered from this through Christ. The church is looking for Christ to come for it before God's wrath is poured out upon the earth. The Lord's Supper reminds us of this wonderful truth.

Finally, as we partake of the Lord's Supper, we get to enjoy the fellowship of the body of Christ. We eat the bread and we drink the juice and we are reminded that God has brought us into a circle of fellowship with him and with his church. We belong to the family of God. We are a part of the bride of Christ that Jesus loves so much and for which he gave himself. This brings sweet comfort to our soul as we observe the Lord's Supper.

When a person is saved and has followed Jesus in baptism, he is then ready to partake at the Lord's table. This is the order in which the ordinances are to be observed. Each ordinance and each observance is a witness to the gospel of the Lord Jesus Christ and to our faith and trust in him for eternal salvation.

**THE ORDINANCES**
**BLOCK 5 - THEME 5 - LESSON 2 (162 OF 216)**
**LESSON OUTLINE**

The two ordinances observed by the church:

**I BAPTISM**

A. An identification
   1. With Christ
   2. With the church
B. An Illustration
   1. Christ's death, burial, and resurrection
   2. The believer's death, burial, and resurrection in Christ
C. By Immersion
D. An Involvement
   1. In the water
   2. In the work

**II THE LORD'S SUPPER**

A. Remembering Christ
B. Proclaiming his death
C. Looking forward to his second coming
D. Fellowship in the body of Christ

**SCRIPTURES TO BROADEN YOUR UNDERSTANDING**

1. Baptism commanded
   Matthew 28:18-20
   Mark 16:15-16

2. Repentance a prerequisite
   Acts 2:38

3. Jesus' baptism
   Matthew 3:13-17

4. Examples of
   Matthew 3:1-6
   Acts 8:38; 9:18; 16:15
   1 Corinthians 1:16
5. The Lord's Supper
   Matthew 26:20-30
   1 Corinthians 11:20-34

**LINES OF THEOLOGICAL CONNECTION**

1. ECCLESIOLOGY
   The ordinances of the church
   Local church membership

2. WORLD RELIGIONS
   Sacraments
   Transubstantiation

3. ESCHATOLOGY
   The second coming of Christ

**THE ORDINANCES**
**BLOCK 5 - THEME 5 - LESSON 2 (162 OF 216)**
**QUESTIONS**

1. How many ordinances do we observe in the Christian church?

2. What are the ordinances we observe in the Christian church?

3. What is the order in which the ordinances are to be observed?

4. List some things that are signified by baptism.

5. List some things we do as we observe the Lord's Supper.

6. Why do we observe these two ordinances?

7. Are you a believer in the Lord Jesus Christ? Have you followed him in baptism?

# 19. A LOCAL CHURCH

## THEME: THE LOCAL CHURCH

BLOCK 5 - THEME 5 - LESSON 3

**LESSON AIM:** Present the church on the local level.

**SCRIPTURE:** (Revelation 1:4)

*"John to the seven churches which are in Asia: Grace be unto you, and peace"*

To this point in our studies, we have learned much about the church. We have learned that the church was a mystery: that is, it did not exist and was a secret in the Old Testament. It was the secret plan of God to use the church to preach the gospel to the world in the event that Israel refused her assignment to do so. The Bible records the fact of Israel's refusal to receive the Messiah, his kingdom, and the mission of world evangelization. Israel was consequently rejected by the Lord and the church, for this time in history, has been given the ministry of reconciliation.

We have learned that the church is the body of Christ in the world today. Christ indwells each believer and desires to live his life through them to take the gospel to all peoples. When believers reach out to others in love and compassion and ministry, it is actually Jesus living through the believer in these ways. He is extending his life and love through ours to reach and win the lost.

We have also spoken of the church in the concepts of universal and local. The universal church is the body of Christ made up of all believers in the church age. Every believer from the birth of the church to the rapture, living or dead, and regardless of denomination or location in the world, is a part of the universal church of the Lord Jesus Christ. The church also exists on a local level. Local could be taken to mean everything from the affiliated churches in a regional area, such as a state or city, or all the way down to the individual church on the corner of Church Street and Main Street in every town in the world. Our focal verse addressed seven local churches. It is the church at this local level that is the topic of this particular lesson.

Considering the local church on the average street corner, we first look at its pattern of organization. Observing any local church, the first thing we would note is its form of government. Government and organization are necessary in order for the church to do what God has put it here to do. There are several options of governmental forms from which the local church may choose from very little organization at all to a highly organized rank and file of hierarchy. Most Baptist churches assume some form of a congregational form of government and organization. This allows the church to be autonomous and gives the membership the opportunity to participate in the decisions that are made in the operation of the church and its ministry.

As we have already noted in a previous lesson, Acts 6 gave us the basic organizational structure of the local church and set the priorities for each group within the organization. The simple organizational structure is that of three groups: pastor, deacons, and the remaining people. The pastors and deacons are the visionary and management portions of the ministry while the larger group of the congregation carries out the daily work of the ministry. The people can be organized to do the daily ministry according to their spiritual gifts as recorded in Romans 12. Every local church organizes itself around some variation of this basic structure.

The next thing we can see as we observe the local church are the people from which the church is formed. In the past in America, local churches were made up primarily of people of the same ethnic background. In the south, that would be mostly what we called white churches and black churches. Today, more and more churches are made up of people from many ethnic backgrounds as the country has become more ethnically diverse. Churches are becoming more inclusive as far as ethnicity is concerned, and rightly so.

While the ethnic background of a local church may be diverse, ethnicity is not to be the deciding factor for church membership. We can simply look at most people and see their ethnic differences, but the thing that really matters is not visible to the naked eye. From the beginning of the church in the book of Acts in the New Testament, the church was made up exclusively of believers in the Lord Jesus Christ. Unbelievers were and are excluded from membership in the local church. They may of course attend but cannot participate in decisions until and unless they make a profession of faith in Christ. Their profession may not be genuine, but they have to make it nonetheless in order to become a member. Only God knows the genuineness of a person's profession of faith. In addition to the profession of faith, a person must follow Christ in believer's baptism in order to become a member of the local church. These are the prerequisites of membership. Other things may exclude membership in a local church such as character or ethical indiscretions, but nothing more is necessary.

Finally, an observance of the local church should reveal its purpose for existing. The purpose of the church can be broken down into a few key areas. First, the church exists to worship the true and living God as revealed in his Son, Jesus Christ. We worship God basically in two ways: through what we call a worship service which includes singing, preaching, giving, praying, and observing the ordinances; and through the deeds we do in the name of Christ. True worship in either one of these areas is contingent upon the attitude of the individual heart of the worshipper.

The church exists to exercise the discipline of its members. When a member exhibits conduct unbecoming of a Christian the church has a responsibility to bring that member into correction. This is necessary due to our greater responsibility to represent Christ in the world. Church discipline is a difficult thing. No one wants to experience it and no one wants to have to do it. It is, however, necessary at times.

The church ultimately exists to fulfill its mission in the world. Jesus commanded his followers to preach the gospel throughout the world and to make disciples of all nations. From a practical stand point, this is the number one reason we exist. Everything we do as a local church should stand or fall on this basis.

It is a privilege to be a member of the church of the Lord Jesus Christ. As its membership, we must accept this privilege and the responsibility that comes with it.

**A LOCAL CHURCH**
**BLOCK 5 - THEME 5 - LESSON 3 (163 OF 216)**
**LESSON OUTLINE**

The local church:

**I ITS PATTERN**
- A. Autonomous
- B. Organized

**II ITS PEOPLE**
- A. Believers
- B. Baptized

**III ITS PURPOSE**
- A. Worship
- B. Discipline
- C. The great commission

**SCRIPTURES TO BROADEN YOUR UNDERSTANDING**
Every book of the New Testament includes something for or about the church. Remember these divisions of the New Testament as you read each book, noting the details of the church as you read.

1. The Gospels and Acts

2. The Gentile-Christian Letters (Romans - 2 Thessalonians)

3. The Pastoral Letters (1Timothy - Philemon)

4. The Jewish-Christian Letters (Hebrews - Revelation)

**LINES OF THEOLOGICAL CONNECTION**
1. CHRISTOLOGY
   Christ's love for the church

2. ECCLESIOLOGY
   The birth of the church
   The organization of the church
   The mission of the church
   The operation of the local church

**LESSON GLOSSARY**
1. Autonomous
   Self-governing

**A LOCAL CHURCH**
**BLOCK 5 - THEME 5 - LESSON 3 (163 OF 216)**
**QUESTIONS**

1. What are the two ways we can think of the church?

2. What form of government do most Baptist churches have?

3. What is a congregational form of church government?

4. What are the two prerequisites of membership in the local church?

5. List three purposes for the local church.

6. Are you a member of a local church?  Where?

7. What is your level of commitment and participation in the support and ministry of the local church?

## 20. AFFILIATIONS

## THEME: THE LOCAL CHURCH

BLOCK 5 - THEME 5 - LESSON 4

**LESSON AIM:** Share the typical affiliations of a local church.

In the previous lesson, we learned that many local churches are autonomous, particularly those of Baptist denominations. That is, they are free to organize and govern themselves in such a way as they deem Biblical and necessary. Autonomy is a blessing in that the local church is free to determine the specific way in which it will seek to fulfill the Lord's commission to make disciples in all nations. The church is absolutely free to decide how they will accomplish this mission and how much organizational structure is needed to get the job done. To this point, churches differ in many ways, one from another.

While the local church is autonomous, it must guard against allowing this blessing to be twisted into the perversion of isolation. In an effort to do things as it sees fit, many a church has ended up separated and isolated from other churches or entities which could help them carry out their mission to the world. Isolation of a church keeps a church from making the impact it could make, stunts its growth, and sets it on a course of decline and death. Isolation can be countered with affiliation.

Local church affiliations can help the church to reach its potential and do its job. A Southern Baptist Church benefits from at least three affiliations. The first affiliation we have is with our denomination, The Southern Baptist Convention. On the National level, the SBC is the largest protestant denomination in the United States. The convention affords us the opportunity to cooperate with other churches across the country to have a share in mission work that we would not otherwise have on our own. Two mission boards are supported by the convention, the International Mission Board (IMB), and the North American Mission Board (NAMB). The IMB provides missional services outside the country, while NAMB promotes missions on the continent. Each one employs and sends missionaries to locales within their jurisdiction. Churches affiliated with the convention get to participate in this work by sending and supporting missionaries, or by working directly with a missionary on mission projects. They also have the opportunity to contribute to special offerings which also go to support this work. These avenues provide ways the local church can enlarge its coasts to make a greater impact in the world.

Most states within the United States have a state convention also affiliated with the national convention. When a state does not have its own convention, it is usually part of a convention made up of several states. In South Carolina where these lessons were written, SBC churches are affiliated with the South Carolina Southern Baptist

Convention. The convention on the state level is there to assist the local church in many ways to be healthy and to fulfill its mission. The convention provides training, support, missional opportunities, and other cooperative efforts to keep churches strong and moving forward for the cause of Christ. Local churches can benefit in many ways from having a vibrant affiliation with the denominational conventions on the state and national levels.

Another great affiliation the local church can have within the Southern Baptist Convention is that of the local association of churches within the state convention. Most counties have their own association of churches or they combine two or more counties or regions to create one association. The association, or network as some are called, is headed by a leader called the Director of Missions. Working with paid or volunteer staff and committees, the associations provide up-close support and opportunities for connections to the local churches within their network. They also communicate convention initiatives to the churches, resulting in much work being done for the Lord through their cooperation with other churches.

Local associations also open the door for local churches to partner with other local pastors and churches in their area. This too is a combatant to isolation. Within the network and in the pastoral conferences, ideas, celebrations, and struggles are shared which let each church know that it is not the only church facing a difficulty of some kind. This kind of openness and transparency creates encouragement and boosts the courage that keep churches pressing onward. The church that does not take advantage of these opportunities to network makes itself unnecessarily vulnerable to isolation and the attack of the enemy upon an easy target.

The previously mentioned are the general affiliations available to every Southern Baptist Church. But these are not all of them. A local church may have as many affiliations as it wants to have or needs to have. Sometimes a local church may find affiliation with other ministries outside their denomination. There may be a local, state, national, or international mission organization, or parachurch group, with which a church may choose to affiliate. Many churches partner with such organizations as Samaritan's Purse, World Vision, Wycliffe Translators, New Tribes Missions, or many, many other good and worthwhile ministries. These are commendable, encouraged, and applauded if God has led the local church to be a part of these great works.

Local churches also find affiliation with a certain pastor, evangelist, or other ministers of the gospel. Churches with strong ties to these ministers both contribute to as well as benefit from the ministries of these individuals or groups. Often times, a church may choose to include support for these ministers and their ministries as a part of their church budget. There is no limit to the kind of or number of affiliations a local church may have.

Affiliations are a great blessing to the local church. In addition to keeping the church from being isolated, they can foster much growth and involvement from members of the churches. However, as with all things, there is a danger that the local church must guard against concerning affiliations. This danger is that the ministry of the affiliation can strongly overshadow or even replace the ministry of the individual members of the local church. The members of a church can become so caught up in giving to a great ministry that is doing great things in the world that it can fall into one of two traps. First, it can think it is relieved of personal ministry obligations since it is helping to finance the work of another. Or, it can give so much to another ministry that it makes it impossible to fund ministry through the members of the local church at home. Either trap is a detriment to the local church. Denominational or other support outside the local church should never take the place of the personal equipping of members of the local church to discover, develop, and deploy their own ministries. God does not give us a pass on personal responsibility, no matter how much money we may contribute to a good cause. We cannot expect to pay someone else to do our mission work for us.

With all of the outside support and cooperation that is available to the local church, there is no excuse for a church to move off to the side all by itself. Churches need the fellowship of the body of Christ. Other churches need the help and support that may come to them through us. This interchange is possible through affiliations with other ministries that are available to and through the local church.

**AFFILIATIONS**
**BLOCK 5 - THEME 5 - LESSON 3 (164 OF 216)**
**LESSON OUTLINE**

Local church affiliations:

**I DENOMINATIONS**
- A. National level
- B. State level

**II ASSOCIATIONS**
- A. Network support
- B. Other churches

**III OTHER AFFILIATIONS**
- A. Ministries
- B. Ministers

**SCRIPTURES TO BROADEN YOUR UNDERSTANDING**

1. Supporting each other
   Colossians 4:7-18

**LINES OF THEOLOGICAL CONNECTION**

1. ECCLESIOLOGY
   Cooperation between the churches
   Support and encourage one another

**AFFILIATIONS**
**BLOCK 5 - THEME 5 - LESSON 3 (164 OF 216)**
**QUESTIONS**

1. What are some affiliations which a local church may have?

2. What does affiliation with other ministries prevent in the local church?

3. Why is the isolation of a local church so dangerous?

4. What is the danger of over-affiliation?

# 21. BASIC BELIEFS OF THE CHRISTIAN CHURCH

## THEME: FRIENDS AND FOES OF THE CHURCH

BLOCK 5 - THEME 6 - LESSON 1

**LESSON AIM:** Share the basic doctrines of the Christian church.

**SCRIPTURE:** Ephesians 4:4-6

4 *There is one body, and one Spirit, even as ye are called in one hope of your calling;*
5 *One Lord, one faith, one baptism,* 6 *One God and Father of all, who is above all, and through all, and in you all.*

The greatest entity in the history of the world is the church of the living God. Unfortunately, not everyone sees it this way. There are many rivals, offshoots, and just plain old foes of the church. The world is filled with religions, cults, and the occult which offer alternatives to the true church of God. With many of them so close to the real thing, how can we tell the difference between the true church and a close second? One of the distinguishing marks of the church is the doctrine it believes and teaches. This lesson will look at the most basic teachings of the true church of the Lord Jesus Christ.

The obvious place to begin with the doctrines of the church is with God himself. The church believes that there is one and only one true and living God. This God identified himself to man as Jehovah. He is the creator and controller of all creation. Before anything else existed, there was only himself. There is none other above him in the earth or in the universe. He is the God of the true church. This fact will go a long way in exposing a false church or religion. If they claim another other than Jehovah as God, you can be sure they are a counterfeit to the church.

The one true God does manifest himself in three distinct persons who are equally God. These persons are God the Father, God the Son, and God the Holy Ghost. Each one is equally God to the other two persons within the godhead. They each have different works to do in working out the plans and purpose of God. The church recognizes each person in the godhead and gives to each one their due reverence and respect.

The true God revealed himself to man and gave him a written record of himself, his purpose, and his plans for mankind. This record came to us over several hundred years as God moved upon men to write his words. We call this record the Bible. We believe the God not only inspired the writings themselves but that he also superintended the collection of the books and their arrangement in the canon of Scripture. The Bible, God's Word, is our guide to living our lives on earth. In it, we learn God's ways and how to live our lives in a way that is pleasing to him. In the Word, we have all things which pertain to life and to godliness. Anything we will ever have to face in life can be addressed from the Scriptures in conjunction with the illumination and guidance of the Holy Spirit who helps us understand and apply the Word to our situations in life.

The Bible also reveals an adversary to God and to his people. This adversary is identified as the devil, or Satan. Satan was once a very beautiful and high ranking angel in heaven. He wanted the worship that was due to God to be given to himself. He managed to convince one third of the angels of heaven to follow him in a revolt against God. They were cast out of heaven into the earth and are also the archenemy of mankind. The devil's goal for man is to steal from him, kill and destroy him if possible. While he can never reach this goal over the entire human race, he can sure accomplish it in the individual lives of people. Satan does his work in the lives of people primarily through his cohorts in darkness, demons. Demons are fallen angels. They are the angels who fell from heaven with Lucifer, Satan's original name. These demons are they with whom we wrestle in the daily spiritual warfare. God did not provide a way of salvation for the angels which fell. Their ultimate future is to be separated from God and tormented forever in the lake of fire. In the meantime, the Christian can have victory over them in this world through the Word of God, the Holy Spirit, and through obedience to God.

The Bible gives us our information about these Christian doctrines. It also tells us about man. Man was created by God from the dust of the earth. He was given charge over God's planet earth. The adversary tempted the man to rebel against God as he had done in heaven. The first man, Adam, did rebel and caused the entire human race to fall into sin. Now, every person is born into the world under the condemnation of God. Furthermore, man, of himself is completely unable to do anything about this condition that exists between himself and God. The good news is that God has done all that is necessary to correct the situation, but man has to come to God on God's terms if this is to be done.

As soon as man fell into sin, God announced that he would do something wonderful which would save people from condemnation. He said that he would send a deliverer to rescue fallen man and to destroy the works of the devil. This deliverer was Jesus Christ, God's Son. He came to the earth and died for the sins of man. His death satisfied all of the just demands of God concerning sin. Now, salvation is available for man to be rescued from the fall. As the news of what God has graciously done for man through the death and resurrection of Jesus Christ is heard, a person receives salvation as the Holy Ghost moves in his heart to help him believe. This belief, or faith in Christ, brings the righteousness of God in salvation. God forgives the sin and declares the person righteous in his sight based upon the work of Christ on the cross.

When a person believes on the Lord Jesus Christ unto salvation, the Holy Spirit makes him a member of the church. The church was brought into existence when Israel rejected the kingdom of God. It is made up of those who have believed on Christ from the Day of Pentecost in Acts chapter two until the rapture of the church. The mission of the church is to carry the gospel to the ends of the earth, making disciples of the nations as they believe. Each believer is to serve the Lord in some specific way in order to accomplish his mandate the church.

Everyone is interested in how the history of man upon the earth is going to conclude. The Bible addresses this subject also. We refer to it in theological terms as eschatology; the doctrine of last things. While there are numerous events and details in the Bible concerning the end of the age, we may generally group them into three categories. First, we have the second coming of Christ to the earth. This will take place in two events, separated by a period of at least seven years. The rapture of the church will occur first followed by the revelation of Christ to the world. The two events are separated by the tribulation and the great tribulation. The Battle of Armageddon will be interrupted by the return of Christ followed by the judgement of the nations.

The second category of events concerns the millennial reign of Christ upon the earth. For one thousand years, Jesus will rule the world from Jerusalem. This will be the final theocracy of the ages. At the end of the millennium, Satan will make his final attempt to overthrow God. His army will be destroyed while he and his followers will be cast into the lake of fire forever.

Finally, the Bible tells us of the eternal state of man. As stated, all unbelievers will spend eternity apart from a God in everlasting torments. The righteous will live eternally with God in a newly constructed heaven and earth. God will be with us and we will be his people. We will live with him forever in the perfect relationship he has always wanted to enjoy with us. We will be free from sin and all that is against God. This is the eternal state of the believer.

These doctrines are the basis of all other teachings in the Bible. Each doctrine named here is a world of study in itself. Our purpose here is merely to mention them in order to show the basic belief of the church of the true and living God. The serious student of the Bible should explore each of these doctrines, seeking the help of the Holy Spirit to understand God's plan for man, both here on the earth at this time and in eternity.

**BASIC BELIEFS OF THE CHRISTIAN CHURCH**
**BLOCK 5 - THEME 6 - LESSON 1 (165 OF 216)**
**LESSON OUTLINE**

**I ONE TRUE GOD**
- A. Jehovah
- B. Triune

**II THE BIBLE**
- A. Inspired of God
- B. The guide for living

**III THE ADVERSARY**
- A. Satan
- B. Demons

**IV MAN**
- A. Fallen
- B. Unable to save himself

**V SALVATION**
- A. By Grace
- B. Through faith

**VI THE CHURCH**

A. Its members
B. Its mission

**VII LAST THINGS**

A. The return of Christ
B. The millennial reign of Christ
C. Eternity

**SCRIPTURES TO BROADEN YOUR UNDERSTANDING**

1. God
   Genesis 1:1
   John 1:1-5
   1 John 5:7

2. The Word of God
   2 Timothy 3:16-17
   2 Peter 1:21

3. The Devil
   Isaiah 14:12-17
   Ezekiel 28:11-19
   Matthew 4:1-11
   Ephesians 6:10-12
   Revelation 20:10

4. Man
   Genesis 1-3

5. Salvation
   John 3:15-16
   Acts 16:31
   Romans 10:9-15
   Ephesians 2:8-9

6. The church
   Matthew 28:18-20
   Acts 1:8
   Acts 2
   Ephesians 2:11-3:6

7. Last things
   Matthew 24-25
   I Thessalonians 4:13-18
   Revelation 19:11-16
   Revelation 20:6

**LINES OF THEOLOGICAL CONNECTION**

1. THE DOCTRINE OF GOD
   The trinity
   The person and work of God the Father
   The person and work of God the Son
   The person and work of God the Holy Spirit

2. THE DOCTRINE OF THE SCRIPTURES
   Inspiration
   Illumination
   Canonization
   Preservation

3. THE DOCTRINE OF SATAN
   His origin
   His works
   His end

4. ANTHROPOLOGY
   The creation of man
   Man's fall into sin
   Man's purpose on earth

5. SOTERIOLOGY
   Salvation by grace
   Faith
   Evangelism

6. ECCLESIOLOGY
   The beginning of the church
   The mission of the church

7. ESCHATOLOGY
   The rapture of the church
   The Revelation of Christ
   The eternal state of man

**BASIC BELIEFS OF THE CHRISTIAN CHURCH**
**BLOCK 5 - THEME 6 - LESSON 1 (165 OF 216)**
**QUESTIONS**

1. Why is doctrine important?

2. Who should be a student of theology?

3. Get yourself a basic theology text book in order to study the doctrines of the church.

4. Research the topics mentioned in the theological connections section of this lesson.

# 22. NON-CHRISTIAN RELIGIONS

## THEME: FRIENDS AND FOES OF THE CHURCH

BLOCK 5 - THEME 6 - LESSON 2

**LESSON AIM:** Show that there are many non-Christian religions in the world today.

**SCRIPTURE:** (1 John 4:1-3)

*1 Beloved, believe not every spirit, but try the spirits whether they are of God: because
many false prophets are gone out into the world. 2 Hereby know ye the Spirit of God:
Every spirit that confesseth that Jesus Christ is come in the flesh is of God: 3 And every
spirit that confesseth not that Jesus Christ is come in the flesh is not of God: and this is that spirit of antichrist, whereof ye have heard that it should come; and even now already is it in the world.*

Jehovah, the only true and living God, is to be worshipped. He created man upon the earth in his own image. One of the purposes for man was that he would worship the true God of the universe. Man has an innate need to worship. In the beginning, man's natural inclination to worship was directed toward God. Since the fall, it has been directed away from God toward other things.

Lucifer, a beautiful and high ranking angel in heaven who was probably a leader of the worship that was offered to God, decided that he deserved and wanted this worship to bc dirccted toward himsclf. Hc and thc angclic cohorts who followcd him in his revolt against God were ejected from heaven into the earth. Lucifer became the devil, God's archenemy, and caused the first man and woman on earth to turn their worship away from God. This fall from God into sin caused the entire human race to fall as well. Man was left with the need to worship, but now, he would worship anything and everything except God. Satan had misdirected man's natural need and desire to worship God.

Satan's hijacking of worship has resulted in man's offering his worship in the wrong directions. Now, man worships the creation over the Creator, and he worships the gods of his own imagination and making. This false way of worship may pacify man but it can never satisfy him because it is a substitute for true and genuine worship offered to the true God. God will not accept this worship because it is not offered to him and it is not offered according to his directions. Satan, in a round-about way, ultimately is worshipped because he is the black-heart behind this robbing God of his worship.

Man was built for worship. He is going to worship something. If he does not worship God, he will find someone or something else to worship. Religion is man's attempt to satisfy his inner need to worship God. The worship of the true God happens in the personal relationship between God and man. This relationship is accurately expressed in most forms of Christianity. Non-Christian religions are satanic counterfeits for worship of the true God.

The study of religion is fascinating, revealing many of the subtle add-ons and take-aways of Satan. Remember that his starting point is the truth. He has to keep a religion close to the truth in order to attract followers, but mixed with just enough error to deceive. For example, in Christianity, Jesus called his followers *witnesses.* The word he used for a witness is the Greek word *martoos.* This is where we get our English word *martyr.* A Christian is to be a living sacrifice for God, denying himself that Jesus might live in and through him, extending the love of God to others. On the other hand, a Muslim is encouraged to physically martyr himself and in so doing, try to kill as many other people as possible. Satan is a master of deceit. We should keep the following facts in mind when studying religions.

Fact number one is that religion is universal. That is, every person born into the world is born with the built-in purpose and desire to worship. This is one of the ways that we bear the image of God. No matter where you go in the world and no matter where you may find people, they will be worshipping something when you first encounter them. This is one of the things that makes it hard for them to receive the truth of Christianity. Their false religion and ways of worship are all they have ever known. To embrace the truth is to deny many things about their heritage and culture.

Fact two is that religion helps people cope with the difficulties of this present life. McDowell and Stewart in *Handbook of Today's Religions* define religion in this way: religion is "that aspect of one's experience in which he attempts to live harmoniously with the power or powers he believes are controlling the world." This may or may not bring peace or hope to the worshipper's life, but in his mind, at least he has tried to do what he thought his god wanted in order to be honored. In this way, he has tried to live in harmony with the god of his religion.

Fact three is that religions are practiced in various ways around the world. These variations may include anything from diets, chants, dances, observances, prayers, or even the offering of animal or human sacrifice. If you encounter those who practice another religion, do not be surprised to learn that the practice of their religion may be much different than yours.

Fact number four is that all roads do not lead to the true God or to his heaven. The true God has revealed himself to man through his Word and through his Son Jesus Christ. He has specified how he is to be approached through the blood of his Son. This is the only propitiation for sin. Man-made religions are the works of Satan which deviate from the Biblical approach to God. In fact, this is the primary way to spot a false religion: ask of it what it believes about Jesus Christ. There is only one road to God and this is the Lord Jesus Christ. All other roads lead to spiritual destruction.

It is presently estimated that there are as many as 4,300 different religions in the world. Some 1,200 of them are found in the USA. All of the main religions in the world trace their beginnings back to the East or to the Middle East. Some of them were in existence before Christianity. A non-Christian religion claims a god other than Jehovah as its Supreme Being. Among the non-Christian religions, out of India came Hinduism and its three best-known offspring: Jainism, Buddhism, and Sikhism. In China, arose Confucianism and Taoism. The national religion of Japan is Shintoism. And out of the Middle East came Judaism, Zoroastrianism, and Islam. These are the major non-Christian religions of the world. Islam is the largest and fastest growing of them all. It is estimated that its numbers will overtake Christianity by 2070.

There are also the religions that are labeled as secular. These religions typically claim no god other than man and the natural world around him. Secular religions include Atheism, Agnosticism, Skepticism, Marxism, Communism, Humanism, and Existentialism. Another category altogether are the tribal religions around the world.

Volumes of books have been written about these and other religions in the world. It would be a stretch to try to read them all and seek to know all there is to know about each one. This would be an enormous, exhausting, and perhaps impossible task. The best thing to do is to know Christianity as well as you can know it. This will help you not only live its truth but will help you identify a counterfeit when it appears.

**NON-CHRISTIAN RELIGIONS**
**BLOCK 5 - THEME 6 - LESSON 2 (166 OF 216)**
**LESSON OUTLINE**

**I WORSHIP GONE WRONG**
- A. Original worship
  - 1. God is to be worshipped
  - 2. Man was created to worship God
- B. The birth of religions
  - 1. Satan hijacked worship
  - 2. Religions are man's attempt to satisfy his need to worship

**II FOUR FACTS ABOUT RELIGION**
- A. Religion is universal
- B. Religion helps people cope with the present life
- C. Religious practices vary
- D. Not all roads lead to God

**III OTHER RELIGIONS**
- A. Non-Christian
  - 1. Hinduism
  - 2. Jainism
  - 3. Buddhism
  - 4. Sikhism
  - 5. Confucianism
  - 6. Taoism
  - 7. Shintoism
  - 8. Judaism
  - 9. Zoroastrianism
  - 10. Islam
- B. Secular
  - 1. Atheism
  - 2. Agnosticism
  - 3. Skepticism

4. Marxism
5. Communism
6. Humanism
7. Existentialism.

C. Tribal

**SCRIPTURES TO BROADEN YOUR UNDERSTANDING**

1. God is to be worshipped
   Exodus 20:1-6
   Exodus 34:14
   Psalm 29:1-2
   Matthew 4:10
   John 4:24
2. Worship perverted in the fall
   Romans 1:18-27

**LINES OF THEOLOGICAL CONNECTION**

1. THE DOCTRINE OF THE SCRIPTURES
   Hermeneutics
   False doctrine

2. THE DOCTRINE OF SATAN
   Satan's perversion of Scripture
   The spirit of antichrist
   The instigator of false doctrine

3. SYSTEMATIC THEOLOGY
   Study all doctrines of the Christian faith

**NON-CHRISTIAN RELIGIONS**
**BLOCK 5 - THEME 6 - LESSON 2 (166 OF 216)**
**QUESTIONS**

1. What is religion?

2. Where do false religions come from?

3. What is one thing Satan may use to start a new religion?

4. What subject is a good test to determine if a religion is true or false?

5. How is a non-Christian religion identified?

6. How are secular religions identified?

7. Where did many non-Christian religions originate?

8. Do all religious roads lead to the true and living God?

# 23. THE CULTS

## THEME: FRIENDS AND FOES OF THE CHURCH

BLOCK 5 - THEME 6 - LESSON 3

**LESSON AIM:** Present the basic identification marks of a cult.

**SCRIPTURE:** (1 John 4:1-3)

*1 Beloved, believe not every spirit, but try the spirits whether they are of God: because many false prophets are gone out into the world. 2 Hereby know ye the Spirit of God: Every spirit that confesseth that Jesus Christ is come in the flesh is of God: 3 And every spirit that confesseth not that Jesus Christ is come in the flesh is not of God: and this is that spirit of antichrist, whereof ye have heard that it should come; and even now already is it in the world.*

The world of Christianity and the non-Christian religions is very complex and confusing. In the beginning, there was the true God. Now, with the aid of demonic doctrines, man has devised a world filled with thousands of religions headed by millions of gods. Of course in reality, these gods are no gods at all. But, they do not have to exist in reality if the devil can get them to exist in the mind of man. And this is what he has done. Now, if this world of Christianity and false religions, and false gods is not confusing enough, add the cults to the mix and see how much more muddy the waters really become.

In a general sense, you might use the following guide to recognize the differences between all of the above. Christianity worships Jehovah, the only true and living God. The non-Christian religions say there is a god but it's not Jehovah. Secular religions say we are pretty sure there is not a true God but the closest thing to it is man and nature. Tribal religions tend to worship spirits. The cults say there is a God but we have the exclusive scoop on him. The occult, which will be the topic of the next lesson, worships anything from nature to Satan himself. Sometimes the lines are blurred between these divisions, but as stated, this can be a general guide.

Perhaps when you think of a cult, you may think of a group of weirdos and misfits who have collected themselves to promote some outlandish idea of man's purpose on earth and how it will all come to an end. For some, this is not far from the truth. However, many of the cults are membered by intelligent, upstanding people who make the greatest neighbors you have ever had. They drive nice cars, live in nice homes, have nice children, worship in nice buildings, are highly organized, and have many followers across the world. What is it that makes them differ in their belief from Christianity, and why are they such a threat to the kingdom of God?

A cult may not always be easy to spot on the surface. Many of them have a form of godliness and seem to be our allies in the faith. However, when we begin to study their beliefs and observe their actions, their cultish nature begins to appear. As a general rule, the cults oppose orthodox Christianity in some way or another. It may not be across the board in every doctrine, but it will usually be in a particular doctrine of the faith. A misinterpretation of the Scripture in one point may often be the seed of the springing up and growth of a cult.

Cults appeal to the vulnerable. They prey on the problems and needs of people, especially the emotionally vulnerable. Their approach may follow a path similar to the following. When a potential member and the way of access to that person's life has been identified, the cult makes sure it is there to answer all their questions and meet their needs. They befriend them and convince them that they are the solution to their problems. At the same time, they may begin to sell them on their view that an apocalypse is coming to the world and they alone are the ones who will be saved from it. They isolate themselves from others in the world for various reasons but at least in one way, to be ready to be delivered from the coming end of the world. To keep their members in the group and under control, a cult goes about to manipulate information and doctrine to keep the group together and on the path. They control many aspects of the member's lives including how much sleep they can have, what they can eat, the clothes they can wear, and where they are allowed to go. They may even keep them in the group by making threats to their lives or to their families. They might even tell them if they do not follow all the guidelines of the group, they will lose their salvation and be left to suffer the coming doom.

In addition to these generalities, the cults move in several specific areas as well. One area is, of course, what it believes about God. Two areas in particular will often stand apart from the orthodox teaching of the faith. The cults may take different stance on the doctrine of the trinity. They may not admit that the one true God lives in three distinct persons; Father, Son, and Holy Ghost. They may attack one or all three of the persons of the godhead. Particularly, Jesus will be attacked. From his deity, to his redemptive work, to his work in the world today, and in the future, Jesus will be presented in some form other than what he is revealed to be in the Scriptures. These areas are dead give-aways to recognizing a cult.

Another specific area of operation for the cults is in the area of the Scriptures and doctrine. The Scriptures are a closed book. However, a cult will often lay claim that it has been given a new revelation from God that he has never revealed to any other person or group. Or, they may present a new interpretation of the Scriptures which is opposed to Biblical, historical Christianity. And beyond this, they may even claim to have extra-biblical revelation that supersedes the Bible. For some cults, the Bible comes in fourth place or beyond in the order of its important writings. As far as doctrine goes, it is constantly changing. Claims the cults make do not come to pass. Explanations are given and the lines in the sand are moved to keep the group in tow. Therefore, Scripture as a guide cannot be trusted. Only the leader of the cult has the answers, and the answers constantly change. This creates a greater allegiance and loyalty to the cult leader.

A last specific area to mention in which cults deal with their followers is in the area of salvation. Naturally, salvation by grace through faith in Jesus Christ is never an option. At best, it is faith in Christ plus something else which brings salvation. Salvation for a cult is based upon some kind of works rather than the grace of God which leads to faith in Jesus alone.

These are some general and specific ways a cult may be identified. While some cults may live in a compound on the side of a mountain, others meet openly in all the major cities of the world. To mention a few groups which are considered cults may be helpful as a place to start in observing the differences between them and the Christian faith. Some known cults are Eastern Mystic Religions, Christian Science, Scientology, Mormonism, Seventh Day Adventists, Jehovah's Witness, The Unification Church, and Wicca. Other cults may be localized and centered around a charismatic leader.

Cults are all around us in every part of the world. Christians should be grounded in the Word of God and in the historical teachings of the Christian church in order to recognize, avoid, and witness to cults members in which we may come in contact. The truth of the gospel of the Lord Jesus Christ is our only defense and their only hope.

**THE CULTS**
**BLOCK 5 - THEME 6 - LESSON 3 (167 OF 216)**
**LESSON OUTLINE**

**I GENERAL GUIDE TO RELIGIONS**

A. Christianity - Worships Jehovah
B. Non-Christian religions - Worships other gods
C. Secular religions - Worships man, nature, or no god at all
D. Cults - May worship Jehovah or not, but with something added
E. Occult - Worships everything from the earth to Satan

**II GENERALITIES OF A CULT**

A. Opposes orthodox Christianity
B. Appeal to the emotionally vulnerable
C. Take an apocalyptic stance
D. Promote isolation
E. Manipulate information and doctrine
F. Control their members
G. Make threats to members

**III SPECIFICS OF A CULT**

A. Relating to God
  1. Oppose the teaching of the trinity
  2. Oppose Jesus Christ
B. Relating to Scripture and doctrine
  1. Scripture
    a. New revelation
    b. New interpretation
    c. Extra-biblical writings
  2. Doctrine
    a. Constantly changing
    b. No stability in doctrine
C. Relating to salvation
  1. No salvation by grace and faith in Jesus alone
  2. Salvation is by works

**IV SOME KNOWN CULTS**

A. Eastern Mystic Religions
B. Christian Science
C. Scientology
D. Mormonism
E. Seventh Day Adventists
F. Jehovah's Witness
G. The Unification Church
H. Wicca.

**SCRIPTURES TO BROADEN YOUR UNDERSTANDING**

1. Study the Word
   2 Timothy 2:15
   2 Timothy 3:14-17

2. Avoid false teaching
   Romans 16:17-20
   1 Timothy 6:3-5
   2 Timothy 3:1-5
   2 John 9-11

**LINES OF THEOLOGICAL CONNECTION**

1. ECCLESIOLOGY
   The doctrines of the church
   Identifying the cults

2. THE DOCTRINE OF THE SCRIPTURES
   Study the scriptures
   Teaching the scriptures

**THE CULTS**
**BLOCK 5 - THEME 6 - LESSON 3 (167 OF 216)**
**QUESTIONS**

1. What are some rivals to the church mentioned in this lesson?

2. What are the general differences between the groups in the previous question?

3. What is the general pathway followed by the cults?

4. List some specific areas of cult beliefs and practice.

5. List some known cults.

6. What is our defense from the cults?

7. Have you ever encountered a cult member? What was your experience?

# 24. THE OCCULT

## THEME: FRIENDS AND FOES OF THE CHURCH

BLOCK 5 - THEME 6 - LESSON 4

**LESSON AIM:** Present the basic identification marks of the occult.

**SCRIPTURE:** (Deuteronomy 18:9-13)

*9 When thou art come into the land which the LORD thy God giveth thee, thou shalt not
learn to do after the abominations of those nations. 10 There shall not be found among
you any one that maketh his son or his daughter to pass through the fire, or that useth
divination, or an observer of times, or an enchanter, or a witch, 11 Or a charmer, or a
consulter with familiar spirits, or a wizard, or a necromancer. 12 For all that do these
things are an abomination unto the LORD: and because of these abominations the LORD
thy God doth drive them out from before thee. 13 Thou shalt be perfect with the LORD
thy God.*

As we have already seen in this block of study, the church has many rivals in the world. These rivals are sometimes found within the church but most certainly outside the church. One of these rivals is the occult. Man has basic questions about life for which he is seeking an answer. We have questions like, "Who am I? What am I here for? How is this all going to end?" Obviously, we should look for our answers to these questions in the church and in the Bible. Unfortunately, many other voices cry out with answers, and not necessarily the answers we need. One of these sources of answers to our questions is the occult.

Like the very air that we breathe, the occult is all around us. We can have access to the occult without leaving our homes. More than likely, every one of us has been exposed to the occult in some way but perhaps we were not aware of it. We should remember that the Christian is to be sober and vigilant in the spiritual warfare. We are to be serious and watchful because we have an adversary who is walking about seeking those whom he may destroy. The occult is one of his weapons of mass destruction.

The first thing to note about the occult is that it moves in the realm of secret and hidden things. There is an air of mystery about it and this is one of its attractions. The word *occult* comes from the Latin word *occultus* which means concealed. Similar to cults, the occult claims its share of knowledge about secret or hidden things. Naturally, people want to be in the know. The claim to the knowledge of secret information draws people, especially those who have an unbridled imagination or curiosity.

The occult world also seeks to project its followers in a realm beyond the five natural senses of man. A claim to a sixth sense is often a thing sought or boasted of among the occult. This would be the ability to see, feel, or know of things beyond the kin of mortal man. Since this ability would be limited to a certain few, the masses of the everyday people are suckered into the influence of such a person with this alleged power or ability. Again, they are seeking answers to their instinctive questions in life and think they have found a legitimate source of answers in the esoteric world of the occult.

Also, in general terms, the occult involves the realm of supernatural forces, namely demons. Demons are real. They are fallen angels. They are at work in the world today. They are the primary opponent that Christians face in the daily spiritual warfare. The occult is caught between two hard places concerning demons. On one hand, they think they can have an amiable relationship with them, invoking their powers over the affairs of man in the natural world. On the other hand, they are in bondage to these evil spirits and become pawns in their hands to do the works of the devil among mankind. Understand that demons are incapable of amiable relationships. Like their master Satan, their aim is to steal, kill, and destroy.

The world of occult practices falls into two categories. One category could be called soft-core occult. Soft-core occult are those things which are just as sinful as the other category, but without the obvious appearance of evil. These are those occult practices where all the labels are pulled off and the bad appears as the good. This is the area of the occult where the unsuspecting person gets caught up through some innocent looking activity. We are exposed to soft-core occult practices many times every day. The non-vigilant believer is easily ensnared in this realm of the occult.

Another category of the occult is thought of as hard-core. These are those occult practices which make no claims to be anything other than pure evil and sinful. They may even go to the extent of worshipping Satan as a god and offering sacrifices to him. Many believers would stay away from this realm of the occult while perhaps not seeing the danger of soft-core occult. We treat this much like standing near the edge of a high ledge on a mountainside. We know how far we should go and do not venture beyond that point for obvious reasons. The adversary, of course, does not recognize such divisions. The enemy is happy to have people involved at any level of the occult. Their ultimate goal is to take a person as far down as possible on the path of destruction and the worship of Satan.

We may ask, "What are occult practices that we should be aware of today?" The text we chose for this lesson names many occult practices. From this text, and with some additions, we find the following among the list of occult practices which are readily available to anyone today. Occult practices include things such as divining, witchcraft, the black mass, fire-talking, fire-walking, hypnotism, white magic, black magic, palm reading, astrology and horoscopes, fortune-telling, Ouija boards, tarot card reading, gazing through crystal balls or other things, attempting to communicate with the dead, zombies, Spiritism, and Satanism which may include animal or human sacrifice. This is not an exhaustive list. There are many other occult practices.

We may be exposed to the occult in any number of ways. Media is probably the broadest means of exposure. We encounter occult practices in the books and stories we read, the movies and television shows we watch, and in some cases, in the music we listen to. Perhaps the most influential means of exposure to the occult would come through a friend or other person close to us. They may be involved in the occult and might seek to expose us and involve us as well. Society at large offers occult exposure through anything from reading your horoscope in the daily newspaper or online, through a fortune cookie at the end of an oriental meal, or by passing a palm reader's or tarot card reader's business on the highway.

When the allies landed on the coast of Normandy in June of 1944, somewhere in the neighborhood of one million mines had been buried along the coastline. Each step for an allied soldier was a potential life-altering explosion. The religious landscape has been mined in much the same way in a spiritual sense by our adversary, the devil. He seeks to destroy us and turn us away from God through everything from diluted Christianity, false religion, cult practices, or occult practices. His goal is to steal, kill, and destroy. While walking through the world is a spiritual minefield, we can be shielded and protected by the truth of God's Word. We should read it, study it, memorize it, and meditate on it regularly. We do not have to fall prey to the enemy.

**THE OCCULT**
**BLOCK 5 - THEME 6 - LESSON 4 (168 OF 216)**
**LESSON OUTLINE**

**I THE OCCULT IN GENERAL TERMS**

A. Secret or hidden things
B. Beyond the 5 human senses
C. In the realm of the supernatural

**II TWO GROUPINGS OF THE OCCULT**

A. Soft-core occult
B. Hard-core occult

**III SOME OCCULT PRACTICES**

A. Divining
B. Witchcraft
C. The black mass
D. Fire-talking
E. Fire-walking
F. Hypnotism
G. White magic
H. Black magic
I. Fortune-telling (Palm reading, astrology and horoscopes, Ouija boards, tarot card reading, gazing through crystal balls or other things
J. Attempting to communicate with the dead, zombies
K. Spiritism
L. Satanism

**IV ENCOUNTERING THE OCCULT**

A. Media
B. Friends
C. Society

**SCRIPTURES TO BROADEN YOUR UNDERSTANDING**

1. Those who practice the occult are an abomination to God
   Deuteronomy 18:12

2. Occult practices are among the works of the flesh
   Galatians 5:20

3. The occult encountered by Paul
   Acts 13:6-12
   Acts 16:16-18
   Acts 19:13-16

4. Renouncing the occult
   Acts 19:18-20

**LINES OF THEOLOGICAL CONNECTION**

1. THE DOCTRINE OF DEMONS
   Their origin
   Their activities
   Their future destruction

2. THE DOCTRINE OF THE SCRIPTURES
   How to study the Bible
   Meditating on Scripture

3. ANTHROPOLOGY
   The works of the flesh

**LESSON GLOSSARY**

1. Esoteric
   Secret

**THE OCCULT**
**BLOCK 5 - THEME 6 - LESSON 4 (168 OF 216)**
**QUESTIONS**

1. What are two general divisions of the occult?

2. What three things characterize the occult?

3. List three ways in which we are exposed to the occult.

4. Give an example of soft-core occult practices.

5. Give an example of hard-core occult practices.

6. Where have you noticed the occult in the community?

7. Have you ever participated in an occult activity? What was it?

8. What should you do if you have any occult items in your possession? (Acts 19:18-20)

# 25. DESIRE

## THEME: THE CHURCH EQUIPPED

BLOCK 5 - THEME 7 - LESSON 1

**LESSON AIM:** God has put a desire in your heart that matches his purpose for your life.

**SCRIPTURE:** (Proverbs 4:23)

*"Keep thy heart with all diligence; for out of it are the issues of life."*

Chuck Yeager is a famous aviator. He became an ace in World War 2 when he shot down five enemy planes in one day. He became the first man in history to break the sound barrier, to fly beyond the speed of sound. He credits his success and survival as a test pilot to his knowledge of the individual systems aboard the aircraft which he flew, be it mechanical, electrical, pneumatic, or hydraulic. He knew every system, what it was designed to do, and what it would cause the aircraft to do if it were not functioning properly. From this knowledge, when he encountered a problem in flight, he was able to trace it to the system and to its source, giving the engineers the ability to make corrections and improvements in the systems, contributing to the safety and reliability of the function of the aircraft. Time after time, he pushed the envelope, risking his life to fulfill his role in aviation history.

Christians can think of themselves in a similar way when it comes to our divine design. God created each one of us in a wonderful and unique way. Like an aircraft of complex design, we are equipped with a number of systems which prepare us for the role God has given us to play in his story, and to fulfill our place in the body of Christ. The lessons of this theme take a look at these systems individually. We begin with the all-important system called desire.

The first thing we can say about desire is that it is a core matter. To be a core matter means that when we speak of desire, we are speaking of the deepest of all matters of life. We have to go to the deepest part of ourselves, the inner man, the heart, if we are to know and understand desire. The problem with most believers is that they have never considered matters of the heart on a deep enough level. Many of us simply do not know what desire is and does for us. We have encountered it, but could not put our finger on what it is or what it is there for.

The Bible tells us that desire is a matter of the heart. Solomon said that the issues of life come from the heart. He also said that God has set eternity in the heart of man. David pulled these matters together into one when he wrote that God can reveal to us the desire of our heart. The idea of the desire of the heart is as follows.

When God created us, he had a role in mind that we would fulfill in his story and as a part of his body, the church. Deep within our heart, the person we truly are, God set a desire that matches his purpose for our life. If we can find, know, and understand this desire, we can find the very purpose for our life on earth. John Eldredge said that desire reveals design, and design reveals destiny.

People often say something like this, "I know God has put me here for a reason; I just do not know what it is." Or, they say, "If God will just tell me or show me what he wants me to do, I will gladly do it." These statements and longings can be satisfied when we find and know the desire of our heart.

We encounter desire in two ways. The first way is through longing. Sometimes, we have those brief moments in life where we feel like we have discovered that thing for which we were made. We have some experience that makes us wish the moment would never end. We say something like, "This is it. This is the thing that feels like life to me." Or, we may daydream about what we think the perfect thing would be to which we could give all of our time and energy. Times like these are times in life when we brush up against the desire of our heart, and the reason for which we were created.

We also encounter desire in a negative way. When true desire is suppressed or never uncovered, we fall for substitutes offered by our adversary in an attempt to satisfy this inner hunger for the life for which we were made. Man is looking for something in which to belong and find meaning and purpose. This is because of desire. Unfortunately, many people never find it, and end up giving their life to something short of God's purpose.

Desire is a core matter of the heart. It takes us into that realm of our true identity and purpose for being on this earth. It is also a clue to us as to what God wants us to do with our life. To find desire is an exercise of paying attention to the things we have mentioned and more. We can look over our life and recall those times of longing and try to determine what it is for which we long? What is that thing makes me feel I was made for? We can look at those times when we are pulled away from God, realizing that the enemy seeks to take us in the opposite direction. If we look at the direction to which the enemy is drawing us and consider what may lie in the opposite direction from that, we may learn something of our true purpose in life. We can also examine this clue to life by asking questions like, "What do I enjoy doing? If I could do anything as a ministry for God, what would it be? If there were no obstacles, what would I love to give most of my time doing? If I could respond to any situation that I see in the world,, what would it be? What about life makes me angry? What issues in life am I concerned about? What can I give myself to and feel like I haven't lost any time while doing it?" Questions like these can open the door to the desire which lies deep within your heart. To search for and find desire is like a treasure hunt. Indeed, when you find it, it is a treasure out of which you can live for the rest of your life.

The desire of your heart is the one thing God wants you to know. Granted, he did not make it all that easy to find. He wants us to want it, to search for it, and to discover it. Paul taught that we are to pray that God will reveal our desire to us. To know it is to discover the purpose God has for our life, our place in the body of Christ, and the works which we were intended to do in life. Practically speaking, nothing else is more important to know after we become a follower of Christ.

As much as God wants us to know the desire of our heart, we have an adversary who is actively seeking to keep it concealed from us. The enemy knows what a threat we will be to the kingdom of darkness if we ever discover God's purpose for our life. In that purpose, we neutralize many of the other weapons the devil seeks to use on us: insecurity, insignificance, worry, doubt, fear, uselessness, despair, and so on. In the purpose of God, we have confidence. We make strides. We make an impact for God in the world. We bring glory to God. We accomplish the works for which we were made. We become invincible. These are the kind of things our adversary does not want us to experience.

The enemy will oppose you and your search for your heart's desire, every step of the way. Be advised that when you embark upon this journey, you are in for both the fight of your life, and the adventure of your life. There is no telling where God will take you around the globe in his purpose. There is no telling what experiences you will have as you seek to discover your heart's desire. Take up the journey. Begin the search. Discover your desire. Live out of it for the rest of your life.

**DESIRE**
**BLOCK 5 - THEME 7 - LESSON 1 (169 OF 216)**
**LESSON OUTLINE**

**I DESIRE**
- A. A core matter
- B. A clue

**II GOD WANTS US TO KNOW OUR DESIRE**
- A. Not easy to find
- B. Can be found

**III THE ADVERSARY OPPOSES YOUR DESIRE**
- A. He seeks to keep it concealed
- B. You are a threat to him when you know your desire and live it

**SCRIPTURES TO BROADEN YOUR UNDERSTANDING**

1. Desire
   Psalm 1:6
   Psalm 16:11
   Psalm 37:3-5
   Proverbs 4:23
   Ecclesiastes 3:11
   Ephesians 1:17-19

**LINES OF THEOLOGICAL CONNECTION**

1. ECCLESIOLOGY
   Our place in the body of Christ
   Our desire

2. THE DOCTRINE OF GOD
   God's purpose for man

3. THE DOCTRINE OF THE DEVIL
   The opposition of the enemy
   The weapons the enemy uses against believers

4. ANTHROPOLOGY
   The journey of life
   Discovering the heart's desire
   Living out of God's purpose

**DESIRE**
**BLOCK 5 - THEME 7 - LESSON 1 (169 OF 216)**
**QUESTIONS**

1. Where is desire found?

2. What is the heart?

3. What can our heart's desire reveal to us?

4. List two ways we can encounter desire.

5. How can you begin to discover your hearts true desire?

6. Why does the enemy seek to keep your desire concealed from you?

7. Have you begun the search for your heart's desire? Have you discovered it yet? What is it?

8. Visit the Billy Graham Library in Charlotte, NC to see the impact one life can make when lived out of the desire of the heart.

# 26. SPIRITUAL GIFTS

## THEME: THE CHURCH EQUIPPED

BLOCK 5 - THEME 7 - LESSON 2

**LESSON AIM:** Every believer has at least one spiritual gift. The gift equips us for our personal ministry for God.

**SCRIPTURE:** (Romans 12:4-6a)

*"For as we have many members in one body, and all members have not the same office: So we, being many, are one body in Christ, and every one members one of another. Having then gifts differing according to the grace that is given to us..."*

Another system in the life of the believer in Christ is that of spiritual gifts. When we became a believer in Christ, the Holy Spirit of God moved into our spirit. God lives within us. We call this the indwelling of the Holy Spirit. When he came in, he gave to us a spiritual gift. The gifts of the Spirit equip the church to function as the body of Christ in the world. The process works in the following way. The church is the body of Christ. The church is made up of many members. God has designed a specific place in the body for each member. God gives each member a spiritual gift in order to function in the place of his design. The spiritual gift is one of God's clues as to our personal ministry for him. If you are a believer in Christ, you have at least one spiritual gift, perhaps more than one. It is needful that you discover your gift and function out of it.

The Bible's key passage on the spiritual gifts is Romans twelve. This chapter names seven categories of spiritual gifts. Anything else that might be called a gift in the Bible will align under one of these seven categories. Again, you have at least one of these gifts. Before we list the seven categories of gifts, let's look at some basic facts about the gifts and some things that can hinder our discovery of our gift.

By way of facts about the gifts, the Bible teaches that a person must be saved in order to have an understanding of the spiritual gifts. The Bible says that the things of the spirit are spiritually discerned and that the natural man cannot understand them. The Holy Spirit is the giver of the gift and controls its operation within us. Every believer receives the Holy Spirit at the moment of regeneration therefore every believer receives his spiritual gift at the same instant as salvation. It could be years, however, before the gift is discovered.

Next, every believer has at least one spiritual gift. It is possible to have more than one spiritual gift and it is even possible to have any one of the gifts at any time. God gives the gift as it pleases him and no believer is excluded. We all have at least one predominate gift in order to have a sense of belonging and the enablement to function as a member of the body of Christ.

A third fact is that operating within our gifts will always produce lasting results. When we try to function outside the realm of our gifts we only get fleshly results which do not last and do not please God. Frustration becomes the result of striving to function apart from the divine enablement. Inward satisfaction only comes from walking in the Spirit.

Number four, the purpose of the gifts is to edify the body of Christ while serving as the body of Christ in the world. While the gift does work to give us a sense of identity and enablement, we are to use it for the benefit of others.

Fifth, the knowledge of each other's gifts helps us coordinate and organize the church for service. The best way to know and understand ourselves and others is to know our gifts. By our gifts, we can know who would best serve to meet a particular need. Additionally, our personalities and responses are conditioned by our gifts. This fact can go a long way in helping to manage relational conflicts.

Six, everything we do should be approached on the basis of our spiritual gifts. This is true not only in the church but also in the home, at work, and in recreation. This will help us face everything on a spiritual level.

Fact number seven, although we do not possess all the gifts, we are commanded in Scripture to do each one of them. More important than the gift is the Gift-giver and if he needs to empower one of us with a gift that we do not normally have, we must be willing to be used of God as he sees fit. These basic facts provide a foundational understanding of spiritual gifts and how the church is to live and function within them.

As we seek to discover our spiritual gift, we see that we may encounter some hindrances along the way. Let's consider some of them now. First, the lack of knowledge and understanding of God's plan can hinder the discovery of our gift. Many Christians do not doubt that God leads them but they do doubt that God leads them according to a plan. God has revealed much of his plan to us in the Bible. Learning of this plan can lead to an understanding of the part God wants us to play in what he is doing in the world. This will lead next into our developing strategies to carry out his work.

Second, rejection of what we know God's plan to be will hinder the discovery of our gifts. God is working in us both to will and to do his good pleasure. He wants us to do his will when we have understood it.

Third, the lack of commitment to the Lord and to the church will hinder the discovery of our gift. Carelessness in regard to our responsibility to the church is a sure hindrance to discovering the gifts. The gifts are designed to be used in and through the local church. If we are not in our place to do our part in service, we will find it nearly impossible to discover our spiritual gift.

Last, unresolved spiritual problems will hinder the discovery of our gifts. Sin in our life and the problems caused by sin have to be dealt with in order to have a more clear spiritual vision. Those who are willing to clean up these areas of their life will be able to better make the discovery of their spiritual gift. A good thing to remember in this regard is that God gives grace to the humble but he resists the proud.

Now, let's list the seven spiritual gift categories which are also called by some, the predominate spiritual gifts.

1. Prophecy - This gift has to do with preaching or forth-telling the Word of God.
2. Serving - This gift is designed to meet the practical needs of the ministry.
3. Teaching - The impartation of the doctrine or teachings of God in the Bible.

4. Exhortation - Encouraging others to live according to God's Word and will.
5. Giving - This gift involves the use of personal and corporate resources for ministry.
6. Organization - The use of administration in planning and executing ministry.
7. Mercy - Identifying with a person's situation as you lead them toward ministry.

These are very broad definitions of these important spiritual gifts. You are encouraged to take a deeper look at them as you seek the gift that God has given to you. Remember that God has selected a place in his body from which you are to serve. The gift equips you to serve in that place which God has chosen especially for you. If you have not done so, begin now to discover your spiritual gift.

**SPIRITUAL GIFTS**
**BLOCK 5 - THEME 7 - LESSON 2 (170 OF 216)**
**LESSON OUTLINE**

**I BASIC FACTS ABOUT THE SPIRITUAL GIFTS**

A. A person must be saved in order to have an understanding of the spiritual gifts
B. Every believer has at least one spiritual gift
C. Operating within our gifts will always produce lasting results
D. The purpose of the gifts is to edify the body of Christ
E. The knowledge of each other's gifts helps us coordinate and organize the church for service
F. Everything we do should be approached on the basis of our spiritual gifts
G. Although we do not possess all the gifts, we are commanded in Scripture to do each one of them

**II HINDRANCES TO DISCOVERING YOUR GIFT**

A. The lack of knowledge and understanding of God's plan
B. Rejection of what we know God's plan to be
C. The lack of commitment to the Lord and to the church
D. Unresolved spiritual problems

**III THE SEVEN PREDOMINATE SPIRITUAL GIFTS**

A. Prophecy - This gift has to do with preaching or forth-telling the Word of God.
B. Serving - This gift is designed to meet the practical needs of the ministry.
C. Teaching - The impartation of the doctrine or teachings of God in the Bible.
D. Exhortation - Encouraging others to live according to God's Word and will.
E. Giving - This gift involves the use of personal and corporate resources for ministry.
F. Organization - The use of administration in planning and executing ministry.
G. Mercy - Identifying with a person's situation as you lead them toward ministry.

**SCRIPTURES TO BROADEN YOUR UNDERSTANDING**

1. The spiritual gifts
   Romans 12
   1 Corinthians 12

**LINES OF THEOLOGICAL CONNECTION**

1. PNEUMATOLOGY
   The gifts of the Spirit
   Empowering the gift

2. ANTHROPOLOGY
   Developing a personal ministry from a spiritual gift

3. ECCLESIOLOGY
   The members of the body of Christ
   Organizing the ministry around the gifts of the members

**SPIRITUAL GIFTS**
**BLOCK 5 - THEME 7 - LESSON 2 (170 OF 216)**
**QUESTIONS**

1. How many categories of spiritual gifts are there in Romans twelve?

2. How many gifts does a believer have?

3. Are we relieved of service if we do not have a particular gift that may be needed in a given situation?

4. Have you discovered which one of the seven gifts in Romans twelve that you have?

5. How are you currently using your spiritual gift?

6. What kind of ministry could you develop out of your spiritual gift?

7. Are you able to recognize the spiritual gifts of other believers? Who and what?

8. Are you helping others to discover their spiritual gift?

# 27. TALENTS - ABILITIES - SKILLS

## THEME: THE CHURCH EQUIPPED

BLOCK 5 - THEME 7 - LESSON 3

**LESSON AIM:** We can use our natural and acquired abilities in service for the Lord.

**SCRIPTURE:** (Colossians 3:17)

*"And whatsoever ye do in word or deed, do all in the name of the Lord Jesus, giving thanks to God and the Father by him."*

We began this theme with the illustration of an airplane and how it has many systems which make it do what it was designed to do. The mechanical system is made up of the parts which move. The electrical, hydraulic, and pneumatic systems provide the forces which make the mechanical parts do their work. Today, we might even add a remote, or wireless system, to the mix. A good pilot is one who knows these systems well so that he can use them to his advantage to operate the plane or to correct it when it encounters a problem. Chuck Yeager was a great example of a pilot who could do this.

Our life is much like the example above. We were designed by God to do a job within his church beginning where we are, extending across the globe and into the generations ahead of us. If we are to fulfill the role God intended for us to have, we need to know the systems with which we have been equipped in order to do our work for the Lord. We have already presented two of these systems; desire and spiritual gifts. In this lesson we will present two other systems which we have at our disposal through which we can do our work for God.

The first thing we need to consider is the ability we have to be able to work for God. This is important because the enemy begins very early in our lives to undermine this area. We may grow up having statements directed toward us like, "You can't do anything! You can't do anything right! You'll never amount to anything in life!" Cruel statements like these rob us of the confidence we have in ourselves just to know that we possess abilities. Ability simply means the quality of being able. We were created in the image of God. The Bible says God is able. Therefore, we are able. That is, we have the capacity to do things. More importantly, we have the ability to do something specific. This specific something is another area in which the enemy will attack. If we can get good at something, it can be used for the glory of God, and this is the last thing our adversary wants. If he cannot prevent our getting good in that area, he will shift our focus so that we are only concerned with getting better at what we do for selfish reasons, using our ability to promote ourself rather than God.

Let it be understood at this point that you are able. You possess the quality of being able. You have the capacity to work for the Lord. If this is an area in which you have received much attack during your life, find comfort in understanding why this has been an area of attack. God put ability within you from the start. It has always been there. The enemy wants to destroy it or to get you to use it for the wrong reasons. He uses every means at his disposal to do this, especially the cutting remarks of other people. Let the fact that you are able be restored in your mind and heart. When you embrace this idea, you are in a position to move toward using your ability for the purposes of God.

It is also important that we understand two types of abilities. They are different and all of us can have and use each one. The first type of ability is natural talent. We are born with talents for certain things. These things obviously are different from person to person. Natural talents can be anything for which we have a gift or a knack. Some have the talent for science and for figuring out the deep laws of the physical universe. Some have a knack for mathematics. Some have the talent to play musical instruments or to sing. Some have a talent for speaking or for writing. Some innately understand the human body and use their talent in the medical profession. Some have the talent for design and for constructing buildings and other structures. Some have the talent to understand mechanics and how things work. We could go on and on with this because the list is endless of the talents with which people are born. God is a creating God. He put within us that propensity to create, and this is found in the natural talents we possess and with which we were born.

Another type of ability is called skills. Skills are the abilities which we learn and practice and get better at doing. A person can learn carpentry skills and become great at it the more he uses and develops these skills. A seamstress who masters her trade can become a sought after provider of clothing or decorative products. A potter becomes a master by developing her skills to the highest quality she can attain. A computer technician can learn and develop these skills into a lucrative industry. All of these examples as well as any others we can think of can be used in ministry for the glory of God.

At this point, we know that we have talents and skills. The question becomes, "How can we use them in the ministry?" The process is simple, involving three steps. First, determine the talents and skills that you have. Pay attention to what you are good at, and at what you enjoy doing. Listen to those who give praise to you work. Think about the areas in which you have a real interest. Consider the things someone has taught you to do that you have picked up and have become better at doing. These things can help you determine your talents and skills.

Next, develop your talents and skills. The old saying goes, "He is a jack of all trades, and master at none." This is a twist on the original statement made by Ben Franklin, one who obviously was extremely gifted and talented. He originally said, "Be a jack of all trades, and master at one." In other words, find that talent or skill that you are really good at and become a master at it. Study it. Practice it. Experiment with it. Know all you can possibly know about it. Be the expert on the subject. Develop it to the fullest potential to which you can take it.

The last step is to deploy your talents and skills in the work of the Lord. Find a place where you can plug in and use that with which God has equipped you. If no ministry exists for which you can use your abilities, start one. Find a place in which to serve. To not do so is to waste your abilities and to squander the opportunity you have to do a work for the Lord. The ultimate idea is to bring all of your equipment into play in your ministry. Use your desire, spiritual gifts, talents and skills together in a personal ministry for the Lord. As you already know, almost anything can be developed into a ministry through which you can make an impact in the world.

Many people are standing by with idle hands, wishing God would hit them with a thunderbolt from the sky and reveal to them some awesome work to which he has called them to do. At the same time, they are standing there with a God-given desire within their heart. They have a spiritual gift given to them by the Holy Spirit himself. They have a natural talent for doing something. They have learned many skills which they could employ in a ministry for the Lord. Yet they are idle. Are you one of these people? Start doing a personal inventory today of all the things with which God has equipped you in order for you to do the works God intended for you to do when he created you. You have what it takes. You can do it. Let's get started.

**TALENTS - ABILITIES - SKILLS**
**BLOCK 5 - THEME 7 - LESSON 3 (171 OF 216)**
**LESSON OUTLINE**

**I ABILITY**
A. Capacity - the quality of being able
B. You are able

**II TYPES OF ABILITIES**
A. Talents
B. Skills

**III USING YOUR ABILITIES**
A. Determine them
B. Develop them
C. Deploy them

**SCRIPTURES TO BROADEN YOUR UNDERSTANDING**

1. Do everything for God's glory
   Colossians 3:17
   1 Corinthians 10:31

2. Your labor is not in vain
   1 Corinthians 15:58

**LINES OF THEOLOGICAL CONNECTION**

1. THE DOCTRINE OF GOD
   God created man in his image
   God chooses our place in the body of Christ

2. PNEUMATOLOGY
   The spiritual gifts
   The indwelling of the Holy Spirit in the believer
   The empowerment of the Holy Spirit

3. ANTHROPOLOGY
   Using your desire, gifts, talents, and skills
   Developing a personal ministry

4. THE DOCTRINE OF SATAN
   Satan's methods of attack upon the believer
   Knowing the enemy

**TALENTS - ABILITIES - SKILLS**
**BLOCK 5 - THEME 7 - LESSON 3 (171 OF 216)**
**QUESTIONS**

1. List the four things with which God has equipped us for the ministry.

2. What is the difference between a talent and a skill?

3. What is your heart's desire?

4. What is your spiritual gift?

5. What are your talents?

6. What are your skills?

7. How are you presently using your equipment in the Lord's service?

8. What ministry could you do which would incorporate all of your equipment for God?

# 28. MENTORS

## THEME: THE CHURCH EQUIPPED

BLOCK 5 - THEME 7 - LESSON 4

**LESSON AIM**: Show how beneficial a mentor can be in our life.

**SCRIPTURE:** (1 Corinthians 11:1)

*"Be ye followers of me, even as I also am of Christ."*

Soldiers going into battle are equipped with the supplies they will need for the work they are to do. In backpacks, bags, and belts, soldiers carry equipment from weapons, to ammunitions, to maps, to communications, food and water. They are ready and sustained for a period of time in which to deploy. Christians and similarly equipped for their deployment in the world to carry the gospel to the nations and to do the work of the ministry. God has equipped each believer with everything he could possibly need to do his work for the Lord. There is absolutely no excuse for a believer in Christ to not be involved in personal ministry.

In this theme, we have surveyed the equipment we have been given with which to do our ministry in the world. God created us for a purpose. He put a desire in our heart which matches our purpose. He gave us a spiritual gift to help us do this work. He also gave us extras such as talents and skills which can broaden our ministry opportunities. In this lesson, we will look at one more thing God has given us to aid us in the work. This is the mentor.

A mentor is another name for a disciple-maker. A mentor has the job of helping a younger or less mature believer become a more effective minister for the Lord. Mentoring is an acquired skill. It is a skill every believer should learn and practice. It is basically taking on the responsibility to help a believer grow enough in Christ to find his ministry and to perform it in the fulfillment of the great commission of Christ to make disciples in all nations. The Bible presents a specific process whereby we can mentor another believer. It gives us a number of examples to study to learn how we can use the process to mentor others as well.

One of the mentoring examples we have in the Bible is that of Philip in the book of Acts. Philip was one of the very first deacons to serve in the church. In Acts eight, we see Philip serving as a messenger and as a missionary. We also see him serving as a mentor and we are given two examples of his mentoring work.

Mentoring is a somewhat popular word in the ministry of our day. It seems we are always looking for a new word or phrase to give to an old concept. In this way, we attempt to package old and trusted concepts with catchy or creative titles to make them more presentable to the public. The use of the word, mentoring, has been around now for several years but the concept has been around for the entire history of mankind on the earth. It actually goes back before this to the Creator himself in pre-time eternity. Mentoring is simply the idea of one person getting out in front of another person or group of people and leading the way. It is the same idea that Paul had when he said, "Follow me as I follow Christ." In our day, the idea has also been called pace-setting. Regardless of what title we may put on this concept, it is simply the work of making or building disciples which is the command within the great commission given to us by the Lord Jesus Christ. To be a mentor is to be a disciple-maker.

In the story of Philip, we see Philip attempting to mentor two different individuals. The first man was Simon the former sorcerer in the city of Samaria. This man who had bewitched the city believed on Christ through the ministry of Philip. We are given in (v13) a look into the process of how things are to work as we impact the lives of people with the gospel. Simon believed, was baptized, and continued with Philip for a period of time. This continuing with Philip is the process of mentoring or making disciples. Waylon Moore refers to this as the "with him" principle where one person spends time with another person to teach him how to walk as a Christian.

The second example of Philip with the eunuch from Ethiopia gives us even more insight into the mentoring process. The two examples together offer two great mentoring principles. The first one is the principle of presence with the disciple. We must spend time with those we intend to mentor. The account of the eunuch tells us what to do during this time we spend with our disciples. The Spirit of God connected Philip with a man who had been making an effort to get to know God. Philip ran up beside him as he was reading from the prophet Isaiah. With a simple question, Philip opened the door to a mentoring relationship. He asked, "Do you understand what you are reading?" The answer given by the eunuch is the foundation of the mentoring process. He said, "How can I, except some man should guide me?" As we spend time with people, we should be guiding them toward the goal of becoming fully devoted learners and followers of Christ. To do this requires that we make a plan that will take the student from being a brand new Christian to the place where he can begin to walk on his own with Christ. When raising spiritual children, we can follow the same pattern of raising our physical children. That process is three-fold: we feed them; they learn to feed themselves; they feed children of their own one day. This is a brief outline toward which we should guide our disciples.

A final note from the text is this. Mentoring does not have to take a very long time. In each of these examples, the time Philip spent was short. He obviously spent more time with Simon than with the eunuch, but neither was a very long time. This can be one of the excuses we use to not mentor another person. We may say there is not enough time for us to build this kind of relationship. We should use whatever amount of time we have to mentor others. The time will vary from person to person. To some, we will be able to give more time than others. Some people will not need as much time as others. They just need someone to get them started in the right direction and they will take the ball and run with it.

Every believer in Christ should entertain two questions in relation to mentoring. The first question is, “Who is my mentor?” A better way to state this might be, “Have I been discipled by another believer in Christ?” The mentoring process is the missing link in the modern church. Today, we hear and read much about mentoring but see little of it in practice. This is the number one cause of the declining condition of the church of today. If you have never been personally mentored, you should ask a trained mentor to disciple you. This will make an exponential difference in your life and ministry.

Another question believers should ask is, "Who am I mentoring?" Ideally, we should be mentored before we mentor another person. But if we have learned and developed enough in our life to take on this responsibility, we should do it. Christ commanded us to make disciples. Period. This command is to every believer without exclusion. God intends for you to mentor other believers. It is in your best interest to learn the process and begin to use it.

God has equipped us with everything we need to fulfill our personal ministry for him. Mentors help us learn to find and use the equipment we have been given.

**MENTORS**
**BLOCK 5 - THEME 7 - LESSON 4 (172 OF 216)**
**LESSON OUTLINE**

**I WHAT IS A MENTOR**

A. A disciple-maker
B. Mentoring is an acquired skill

**II PHILIP, THE MENTOR**

A. Philip mentored Simon of Samaria
B. Philip mentored the eunuch of Ethiopia

**III TWO MENTORING PRINCIPLES**

A. The principle of presence
B. The principle of guidance

**IV. TWO QUESTIONS FOR EVERY BELIEVER**

A. Who is my mentor?
B. Who am I mentoring?

**SCRIPTURES TO BROADEN YOUR UNDERSTANDING**

1. The disciple-making strategy
   John 17

2. The discipling of Paul
   Acts 11:25-26

3. The discipling process in action
   Matthew
   Mark
   Luke
   John

**LINES OF THEOLOGICAL CONNECTION**

1. CHRISTOLOGY
   Jesus' strategy of building disciples
   The great commission

2. DISCIPLE-MAKING
   Biblical examples of disciple-making

**MENTORS**
**BLOCK 5 - THEME 7 - LESSON 4 (172 OF 216)**
**QUESTIONS**

1. What is another name for mentoring?

2. What is mentoring?

3. What two mentoring principles do we find in the example of Philip?

4. What is the principle of presence?

5. What is the principle of guidance?

6. Who is expected of God to be a disciple-maker, or a mentor?

7. Have you been mentored to the point of spiritual reproduction? If so, by whom?

8. Are you mentoring anyone presently, or have plans to do so in the future?

## 29. YOUR DREAM

## THEME: A PERSONAL MINISTRY

BLOCK 5 - THEME 8 - LESSON 1

**LESSON AIM:** Your dream is the seed of your personal ministry for God.

**SCRIPTURE:** (Ephesians 3:20-21)

*20 Now unto him that is able to do exceeding abundantly above all that we ask or think,
according to the power that worketh in us, 21 Unto him be glory in the church by Christ
Jesus throughout all ages, world without end. Amen.*

God rescued us from the penalty of sin through the death and resurrection of the Lord Jesus Christ. His salvation includes life with him where he is for eternity. It also includes fellowship with him now in the work he is doing to take the story of salvation through Jesus Christ to all peoples of the earth. It is for this purpose that we have been saved and sent into the world on mission with God.

Every believer in Christ has been called for the same purpose. Every believer in Christ should be engaged in a personal ministry for Christ as we go about fulfilling the purpose for which we have been saved. Many Christians plug into a ministry that is already going on, giving little thought to beginning something new and something tailored to their personal gifts, talents, abilities, skills, and desires. This is fine if it is getting the job done and if we can be content with it, but we should also be open to the possibility that God might want us to begin a totally new ministry, perhaps something no one else has done. An idea for a ministry like this comes from God and is planted deep within our heart. We might call it our dream. It is actually the next step beyond desire. Our dream is what we would do with our desire if there were no obstacles in the way to prevent its coming to pass.

A dream for a personal ministry is not a fantasy or some half-cocked idea that we throw together on a whim. It is not some mystical revelation that we think we have from God because we dreamed one night of seeing a light that led us out of some long, dark tunnel, or something of the sort, and it must mean that we are to do something for God because of it. A dream for ministry is more the development of processed information. It is the conclusion we get when we have considered all the factors involved in our life on earth from God's point of view. When we get a grasp on the story God is telling in the Bible, and when we begin to understand that God wants us to join him in his work, and when we know that he has equipped us with all the tools we will need to fulfill the assignment he has given to us, we can begin to put together a plan to obey the Lord out of the unique way that he has put us together. Our dream for a personal ministry can be something as unique and different as are our fingerprints from one person to another.

Let's take the process we have just mentioned and consider it as we think about our dream for ministry. First, if we are to know what we are to do in the world, we have to know what God is doing in the world. Our life here and now only makes sense as it relates to God. To live apart from God, or as if he does not exist at all is to deny the very reason for our being alive. It is in him that we live and move and have our being. To forget God is to lose all meaning to life. If we truly want to know the meaning of life, we have to start with God. God is telling his story to us, generation after generation, through the Bible that he has given to us. We have to read it and process it for ourselves in our own minds in order to know what God is doing in the world. Since God's aim was to reveal this very thing to man through his Word, it is possible for us to find it and know it from the Bible. When we know what God is doing, we can also know what we are to do with our lives upon the earth also. The thing God is doing is the foundation and framework for what we are to do with our lives. Coupling our life to his is the secret to life, to real living, to satisfaction, to meaning and purpose.

When we know what God is doing and what we are to do, we can join God in his work where he is working in the world. Make no mistake about it, God is at work in the world. He is working according to his plan which is also revealed to us in the Bible. He is working in all of the details of all peoples, governments, and activities upon the earth. He is working through the Holy Spirit to energize the church for its mission in the world. He is working through individual believers to do his will in and through their lives. No one can read the Bible and conclude that God is not at work in the world today.

Since God is at work, we have to be at work as well. God saved us that we might join him in his work. We have to look around for the evidence of God at work and join him where he is and in the work he is doing. To do this will require that we will have to do some things that we might not want to do. It will mean that we have to go to some places where we do not necessarily want to go. It may mean that we have to take some very serious risks when we join God in his work. It will mean that we will have to adjust how we use our money and resources so as to include the work of God in our funds. To join God in his work will be a life-altering experience.

We can join God in his work because he has designed us in such a way that we can do this. We can sharpen our vision so that we can recognize where God is at work so we can join him there. Vision can be defined simply as getting on our heart what God has on his heart. When we see where God is working and among whom he is working, we can be sure that this is something that he would be pleased to have us join. All the many ways God has equipped us prepares us for the work wherever it is and whatever it is. And, if we are lacking a piece of the equipment to do the job, he can either give it to us, or bring it to us in another person whom he would have to join us in the work.

The last thing we have to do after surveying all the information and getting things in the proper order is to develop our dream for ministry. All of the preceding information is the framework for our dream. It is the laying of the tracks on which our dream can run to help us do our personal ministry for the Lord. What is your dream? Do you have an idea for a personal ministry that you would like to do for God? Our focal verses encourage us to dream our best dreams, think our best thoughts, and use our best words as we think about what we can do with and for the Lord. When we do this, he will go exceeding abundantly above all we have asked or thought of in the pursuit of joining God in the work he is doing in the world.

When you have developed your dream to the point of doing it, this is obviously what you have to do next. To have a dream and not do it, never brings the dream into reality. You have to actually put it into practice. Then, you have to continually work it and develop it to see if it will become all you wanted it to be and more. You must not give up on it if it does not immediately produce what you thought it would. You may have to think some more, pray some more, adjust some more, to bring your dream into reality. It can be done. The world does not need you to do the same old thing everybody else has done. The world needs you to be the person God made you to be and to do the work God gave you to do. This can happen if you will follow that dream that God has put within your heart. Are you willing to take the chance?

**YOUR DREAM**
**BLOCK 5 - THEME 8 - LESSON 1 (173 OF 216)**
**LESSON OUTLINE**

**I GOD'S STORY**
A. What God is doing
B. What we are to do

**II WE ARE CO-LABORERS WITH GOD**
A. God is at work
B. We are to work with God

**III GOD HAS BUILT US FOR THE TASK**
A. Vision
B. Equipment

**IV WHAT IS YOUR DREAM?**
A. The framework
B. The fulfillment

**SCRIPTURES TO BROADEN YOUR UNDERSTANDING**

1. God is at work
   John 5:17
   John 9:4

2. We are laborers with God
   1 Corinthians 3:9

3. Read the story of Joseph's dream
   Genesis 37-50

**LINES OF THEOLOGICAL CONNECTION**

1. ANTHROPOLOGY
   The desire of your heart

2. PNEUMATOLOGY
   Spiritual gifts
   Indwelling the believer
   Empowering the believer

3. ECCLESIOLOGY
   Members of the body of Christ

**YOUR DREAM**
**BLOCK 5 - THEME 8 - LESSON 1 (173 OF 216)**
**QUESTIONS**

1. What is the description of a Godly dream?

2. What can God do with our dreams?

3. What should our dream for ministry consider?

4. What is the one thing we should never do with a dream for ministry?

5. Where does a dream for ministry come from?

6. Do you have a dream for ministry? What is it?

7. Have you tried your dream for ministry?

8. What did you learn?

## 30. THE CALLING

## THEME: A PERSONAL MINISTRY

BLOCK 5 - THEME 8 - LESSON 2

**LESSON AIM:** The call to salvation presumes a call to serve God in some way.

**SCRIPTURE:** (Romans 8:29-30)

29 *For whom he did foreknow, he also did predestinate to be conformed to the image of his Son, that he might be the firstborn among many brethren.*
30 *Moreover whom he did predestinate, them he also called: and whom he called, them he also justified: and whom he justified, them he also glorified.*

Much is made among Christians about a call to ministry. The general thinking is that of those whom God saves, he only invites certain ones to join him in his work. Those who are uninvited are free to live their life without any responsibility for the work at hand. These unengaged Christians often rationalize by thinking something like, "Well, if God calls me to do something, I will do it, but until he does, I'll stay on the fringes of Christianity." The Bible does not indicate in any place that some Christians are left out of the work. In fact, it indicates the opposite: all believers are saved so that they might be sent to the work.

In this lesson, we will consider four facts about the call of God upon the life of a believer in Christ. The first thing is that God calls us unto salvation in Christ. The call to receive Jesus Christ as Lord and Savior of our life is extended to us through the sharing of the gospel. When another person tells us the good news that Jesus died on the cross in order to put away our sin from the sight of God, and that he arose from the dead, this presentation is the call of God to us to be saved. When we do believe and receive the gospel, the Holy Spirit does the work within our spirit to help us embrace Christ Jesus and the gospel. We call this transaction the new birth, and specifically the work of the Holy Spirit in regeneration. When the gospel is shared, God is calling the unbeliever to believe and to be saved.

The next thing we need to know about the call of God is that the call to salvation presumes a call to service. That is, from a practical standpoint, we are saved to serve. It is preposterous to think that service to God after salvation is optional. Service is part of the call itself. The question is not, "Is God calling me to service?" The question is, "What service is God calling me to do?"

We might think of the service to which God calls us in two categories. The first category of service we might call standard ministry. By the way, the words, service, and ministry, are interchangeable. Standard ministry is the things that God intends all Christians to do. These include evangelism, disciple-making, church attendance, supporting the church financially, and giving a general Christian witness for Christ where ever we go. God does not extend a special call for us to do these things. These things are not spiritual gifts, embarked upon only by the specifically gifted. These things are that which every Christian is expected to do. They come as part of the package of being a believer, a part of the church, and a witness for Christ.

A second category of service can be thought of as specialized or specific ministry. These are the areas of service which require special training and more sacrifice on the part of the servant. Specialized ministry includes the Christian vocations we normally think of such as pastoral service, missionary service, music ministry, student ministry, and so forth. Specialized ministry can also include parachurch ministry, or non-profit Christian ministry, or whatever we may call doing a ministry and making a living from it at the same time.

How can we know that God wants us to do a specific ministry for him? Will he appear to us in a burning bush, or will he allow us to see him sitting on his throne and giving us a special commission to part waters or to topple the kingdoms of the world? Surely God will call us in some miraculous way if he wants us to do a specific ministry for him, won't he? What we think of as a call from God to specialized service is the guiding of God in our life deeper into the purpose and work he has designed us to do. It happens in the relationship we enjoy with God on an individual basis. It is simply God bringing us to the place in our life where we begin to do the things God had in mind for us to do when he created us.

God is willing to use anyone who will make himself available for God's use and have no reservations as to what extent God may use him. In a sense, standard ministry is the training ground for those who are willing for God to use them in a specialized ministry of some kind. If a person is not faithful and consistent in standard service, how can he be counted on for specialized service? As believers serve faithfully in the standard ways, there sometimes comes a desire to do more for God, to serve him in a greater, maybe even a more sacrificial way. The wrestling over the decision to do more, or to go deeper and farther with God is accompanied by the presence of God during the process to guide our thinking and footsteps. If we are walking with God, he will guide us into the specific work he wants us to do for him. The decision will not always be an easy decision to make. It may take years to make it. It may come after a lot of sleepless nights of prayer and soul-searching. This process of seeking, asking God's guidance, waiting, surrender and decision are what we must go through as we consider the depth of God's call to us in salvation. His call to salvation is a call to serve. The question is, "How far am I willing to go with God?"

God calls us to salvation. A call to salvation is a call to service. The third truth about the call of God is that God calls all of us to the same general task. God is going about his work of taking the gospel of Jesus Christ to all people groups of the world. As people from these groups become believers, we are to teach them how to walk with God and to also join him in his work. This task is what we call the Great Commission. Every believer is called to do the great commission. Every believer is called to be a maker of disciples. This is the first piece of the puzzle of determining our service to God. We have to understand the work we are to do. When we understand this fact, we can then begin to find the specific way God would have us as an individual to do the work. This process will lead us into standard and specialized ministry for God.

Finally, we can know that the call of God is never rescinded. He never takes it back or changes his mind. He has called us to do the work. Until Christ returns for his church, we are to do this work. Of course, the ministry God leads us to perform should grow and develop over time. It should become more than it is when we first begin to do it. But, there will never be a time when God will tell us to forget about it. He is working to bring the nations to Christ. He has called us to join him in his work. We must stay on mission as long as he leaves us here to work with him and for him.

Are you a believer in Christ? Then, God has called you to salvation. Since he has called you to salvation, he has also called you to serve him. He has called you to serve him in the fulfillment of his commission to make disciples of all nations. He wants you to serve him in this purpose in a specific way. He is willing for you to serve him as deeply as you are willing to serve. All of these things are revealed to us in the Bible. You do not have to wait on a lightning bolt to strike you on the head for you to begin your service for God. If he saved you, he also called you to serve. Are you serving?

**THE CALLING**
**BLOCK 5 - THEME 8 - LESSON 2 (174 OF 216)**
**LESSON OUTLINE**

Four facts about God's call:

**I GOD CALLS US TO SALVATION**
A. Through the gospel
B. By the Holy Spirit

**II THE CALL TO SALVATION IS THE CALL TO SERVICE**
A. Standard ministry
B. Specialized ministry

**III WE ARE CALLED TO THE SAME PURPOSE**
A. God's general purpose for all of us
B. God's specific purpose for each of us

**IV GOD NEVER RESCINDS HIS CALL**
A. The call remains
B. The ministry should develop

**SCRIPTURES TO BROADEN YOUR UNDERSTANDING**

1. Isaiah's call
   Isaiah 6:1-13

2. The call of God
   Romans 8:29-30
   Ephesians 4:4
   Romans 11:29

3. Look up the stories of how God called these people:
   Gideon, David, Amos, Jonah

**LINES OF THEOLOGICAL CONNECTION**

1. THE DOCTRINE OF GOD
   God's global cause in Christ
   The Great Commission

2. PNEUMATOLOGY
   Regeneration
   Illumination
   Guidance
3. ANTHROPOLOGY
   Life's purpose
   Finding and fulfilling life's purpose

**THE CALLING**
**BLOCK 5 - THEME 8 - LESSON 2 (174 OF 216)**
**QUESTIONS**

1. How is the call to ministry connected to salvation?

2. What is God's general purpose for all of us?

3. Have you discovered God's specific purpose for your life?

4. Will God ever take back his call on your life to service?

5. Give some examples of standard ministry.

6. Give some examples of specialized ministry.

7. How would you grade your performance in standard ministry at the present time?

8. Is there a specialized ministry that you are considering doing for God? What is it?

# 31. PREPARATION FOR MINISTRY

## THEME: A PERSONAL MINISTRY

BLOCK 5 - THEME 8 - LESSON 3

**LESSON AIM:** Service for the Lord requires preparation.

**SCRIPTURE:** (Mark 3:14)

*"And he ordained twelve, that they should be with him, and that he might send them forth to preach,"*

There is a famous saying that preacher boys often hear when they announce that they think God is calling them to be a preacher. They are told, "A call to preach is a call to prepare." This is true not only of the preaching ministry, but of everything else that can be made into a ministry for God. Our focal verse underscores this great truth. Before God sent the disciples into ministry for him, he drew them close to his side for a period of time. He does the same for his ministers today. This period of time close to the side and heart of God is when he prepares us for the work he has planned for us to do.

The first thing you must do in starting a new ministry is to develop your idea. The idea you have for ministry is your dream we talked about in the last lesson. Simply put, it is that thing that you feel that God wants you to do for him. Once you know what you are to do, development of this dream, or idea, or calling, or whatever else you may choose to call it, begins with making sure it is connected to God's general purpose. He has invited us into the work of making disciples of all nations. The ministry we do must have this as its ultimate goal. To strive for anything else is to engage in a misguided ministry. We have to be clear from the start where we are going. Establishing the purpose of our work at the beginning will keep us on track, preventing many distractions that can spring up along the way. This is not to say that we will never be distracted but it is to say that many distractions can be eliminated altogether when we begin our ministry, and continue our ministry from the right perspective and toward the right goal.

Once we are anchored in the purpose for our ministry, we can then make the plan we need to carry out the work. The thing to remember about a plan is that it is a work in progress. More than likely, things will occur that we did not anticipate or see coming when we made our plan. Or, we will begin to work our plan, and practical experience may reveal a better way to do our work than we first conceived. This is perfectly alright and should be expected. It is when we are unwilling to adjust our plan to allow for wisdom and reality that we set up ourselves to fail. We must pay close attention to the plan we make, identifying the parts of the plan that work as we expected, or better than we expected, or that do not work at all. Being honest with ourselves about the results we get as we work our plan will help us to build the best ministry we can build for the glory of God.

The next thing to do in preparation for ministry is research. We have a dream. We have an idea for a great ministry to do for God. Now, we have to determine who will be the target recipients of this work and where will we have to go to do the ministry we have received from the Lord? As we consider these details, we have to remember that ministry is for the Lord but it is to people. The ministry we do should not only satisfy the need of our life to serve and contribute, but it must also meet the needs of others, or solve a problem in some way. The ministry has to actually do something to help the cause of Christ if it is to be a viable work for God. So, we have to research, who are the people who need the ministry I can provide, and where are they to be found? This research will identify the people who can benefit from our work and the places where the opportunity exists for us to serve. The thing this can lead into is the possibility of uprooting yourself and your family to go to another place to do ministry. This is not always the case, but it can be. We have to know it is a possibility and we must be willing to make a decision to move if God leads us in that direction. As we do our research, and as we begin to do the work, God will reveal to us if we can do the work from where we are or if we need to relocate.

Finally, in order to prepare ourselves to do the best job we can do in our ministry for the Lord, we have to educate ourselves in the field in which we will serve. We need to become the best we can be in the area in which we will work. This means that we will have to study in one way or another. Informal education is certainly a step that every servant of the Lord can and should do in preparation for ministry. Books are available to read and study on most fields from which we choose to work. Similar ministries or services may already exist that we can observe. People may already be engaged in some form of the work that we can talk to and get first-hand experience. We may even step out to try the ideas we have on a small scale to gain information we need to help us develop our ministry. With all of these opportunities available, there should be no excuse for not being prepared with at least some of the knowledge we will need to begin our ministry for God. And we should remember that we do not have to reinvent the wheel, as they say. We can build on the advances others have made by wisely incorporating what they have learned into our work.

Of course, formal education is also a possibility to consider. In fact, for some fields, there will be no possibility to do the work without formal education. This is part of the process. We should not shrink back from something God has put into our heart when we see that it may take years to get the education we need to do the work. The work will wait. All the education we can get will be used on the field, and in some cases, will not even be enough to prepare us for the experiences we will have.

Schools also open a world of networking that proves beneficial as we go to our places of service. When we do encounter those experiences for which we are not prepared, God may remind us of a person we met, or of a school that exists, or of another ministry that is at work which all can become allies for us as we do our work. The truth that no man is an island is continually restated as we venture into the world of the ministry which lies ahead. We need each other and we should call on others when we need the help. This is the way the body of Christ serves to help itself in time of need. And, we have to be willing to be a resource for others when they need us as well. There will be times when God will use you to provide the next step for someone else to take in their work.

Preparation is much of the battle for having a successful ministry for God. As important as it is, however, it is never a substitute for walking with God and depending upon the Holy Spirit for the daily guidance that we need. The Bible tells us that it is not by might, nor by power, but by the Spirit that God does his work through us. All the preparation in the world will never replace the work of the Spirit in our lives. At the same time, we cannot disregard the need to prepare. God's Word stresses the need for preparation as well as reliance upon the Spirit of God. The Spirit uses the preparation when it is there, and makes up for it when it is not there. Both are necessary in the work of the ministry for the Lord.

Where are you in the process of preparing for your work for God? Hopefully, this lesson will help you identify a good starting place for your ministry.

**PREPARATION FOR MINISTRY**
**BLOCK 5 - THEME 8 - LESSON 3 (175 OF 216)**
**LESSON OUTLINE**

**I DEVELOP YOUR IDEA**
A. Connect to the purpose
B. Develop your plan

**II DO YOUR RESEARCH**
A. The people you will serve
B. The locations of the people

**III EDUCATE YOURSELF**
A. Informally
B. Formally

**SCRIPTURES TO BROADEN YOUR UNDERSTANDING**

1. Prepare for the work
   Mark 3:14

2. Paul's example of not being prepared
   Acts 9

3. Study
   2 Timothy 2:15
   2 Peter 3:18

4. The Word of God prepares us
   2 Timothy 3:16-17

**LINES OF THEOLOGICAL CONNECTION**

1. PNEUMATOLOGY
   The Spirit empowers us for ministry

2. ANTHROPOLOGY
   Preparation for ministry

3. THE DOCTRINE OF THE SCRIPTURES
   God's Word prepares us for our ministry

**PREPARATION FOR MINISTRY**
**BLOCK 5 - THEME 8 - LESSON 3 (175 OF 216)**
**QUESTIONS**

1. What is the ultimate goal of every ministry?

2. What should we do as one of the first steps in preparing for ministry?

3. What is an important thing to remember about a plan?

4. What two things can contribute to failure in ministry?

5. What two important things should we learn as we research our ministry?

6. What form of education should all ministers engage in?

7. What form of education is often necessary in order to perform some ministries?

8. Research the Christian colleges and universities in your state. Note the fields of service for which they can prepare you. Does one of them catch your eye?

# 32. MINISTRY PRACTICE

## THEME: A PERSONAL MINISTRY

BLOCK 5 - THEME 8 - LESSON 4

**LESSON AIM:** Put your ministry to work.

**SCRIPTURE:** (Colossians 3:17)

*"And whatsoever ye do in word or deed, do all in the name of the Lord Jesus, giving thanks to God and the Father by him."*

The church is made up of many different members. Each person is a member of the body and has a particular function, an important role to play in the work. God has chosen our place in the body and the work we are to do in that place. Therefore, each individual Christian should be engaged in personal ministry of some kind. We have spent a great deal of time in these lessons sharing the things with which God has equipped us to do the work he wants us to do. It is time now to put all of this together and begin our service for the Lord. We have talked about it long enough. We have analyzed it in great detail. Now it is time to put your ministry to work.

A simple pattern which works in just about any situation will work for us as we begin our ministry for the Lord: practice and performance. We will want to get our ministry off to a good start by following this pattern. First, take your ministry for a trial run. You have spent a lot of time discovering how God has equipped you with spiritual gifts, abilities, talents, and skills. You have considered the desire of your heart. You have determined your dream ministry to do for God. You have connected it to God's purpose of making disciples of the nations. You have developed a plan to put it into practice. You have researched the people and places where your ministry is needed. You have gotten the education you need to help you begin to do your work. It's now or never. Why not take it for a spin?

Taking you ministry for a trial run can be done in a number of ways. You might first want to attempt it on a small scale. This will give you some idea if you are on the right track with how you plan to put your ministry into action. The small scale should provide you with just enough data to help you make any initial adjustments that might be necessary. This can save you much time and resources when you finally launch your ministry. It can also let you know if you have left any bases uncovered and give you time to make these adjustments before you begin full swing.

Another way to take your ministry for a test drive is to join with other ministries of a similar nature, putting your ideas into practice to see how they will perform. This can be done on a short term mission trip or in conjunction with a ministry at your church or in your local area. Most people will be glad to have you come along side of them in their work when they know that you are seeking to launch your own work. They are happy to share their experience with you, becoming an example and maybe even a mentor for you as you begin. This also opens the door for you to learn much as you watch them operate in their ministry. It can help you prepare for the experiences you will have as you get fully engaged in your personal ministry for God.

You might also want to try something on you own as you try out the ministry on a small scale that God has given you. You may identify a small group of people and a local place where you can give your ministry a go. This will give you some personal experience with doing the work, encountering situations, and making decisions as you go. There is nothing quite like doing something for yourself to prepare you to do the work. It can be grievous and intimidating at first. It can make you feel inadequate or that you have bitten off more than you can chew. These feelings must be overcome. These feelings are the subtle ways that the enemy uses at first to try to keep us from fulfilling our destiny. This is another good reason to try the ministry at first on the small scale. It can flush out the enemy, giving you an indication of where you greatest attacks will come from as you go about your Work for the Lord, preparing you to face the greater attacks of the adversary in the future.

When you think you have had enough test driving of your ministry, it is time to launch it and let it do its work. It is time to let it perform. You will get results from the work that you do. They may or may not be the results you anticipated. This is ok. The results you get are not always bad. They may be much better than you expected. Whatever the results may be, they are the data that you use to make any adjustments you may need to make in performing your ministry.

The next thing you do after your ministry has had enough time to produce some results is to evaluate everything you have done and everything that has resulted to this point. The evaluation process looks like this.

1. Attempt
   Put the idea into action.
2. Assess
   Evaluate the effort to see if you are getting the desired results.
3. Admit
   Be honest about the results you find.
4. Adjust
   Can you make any adjustments to the effort to get the results you want?
5. Apply
   Implement the adjustments.
6. Again
   Repeat these steps until the effort works like you want it to work. When an effort no longer serves its purpose, it is time to eliminate it.

This process should get your ministry up and running. The evaluation process will help you adjust your work until you either get the results you desire, or until you realize that you need to abandon the idea altogether. Remember that when an idea does not work, it is not always that it is a bad idea. Sometimes it is just not the right time for the idea, or the idea needs to be used in a different place.

When your ministry is operating as you wish, keep it going. Continue the ministry either until it is no longer needed, or until God leads you to do otherwise. It is always good to try to get the most out of a ministry but remember too, that if it is not broken, don't fix it.

The reality of it all is this: you could be sitting on a spiritual gold mine with the ministry idea that God has given to you. You will never know if it will work, or what God might do with it if you do not put it into action. If you try it, it just might work. If you do not try it, it certainly never will work.

Everything you attempt to do will not be successful. You should know this. But you should not let the fear of failure keep you from attempting great things for God. And, it is not always that a ministry must succeed in order for God to be glorified. The mere fact that God put something in your heart and you tried to act upon it goes a long way with God as well. You really have nothing to lose and everything to gain if you will put your ministry idea into action. What else are you waiting for?

**MINISTRY PRACTICE**
**BLOCK 5 - THEME 8 - LESSON 4 (176 OF 216)**
**LESSON OUTLINE**

**I TAKE YOU MINISTRY ON A TRIAL RUN**

A. Start on a small scale
B. Work with others
C. Try it yourself

**II LAUNCH YOUR PERSONAL MINISTRY FOR GOD**

A. Put your idea into action
B. Evaluate it
C. Continue it

**SCRIPTURES TO BROADEN YOUR UNDERSTANDING**

1. Paul joined with Barnabas
   Acts 11

2. Luke joined with Paul
   Acts 16

3. Do your ministry
   Ephesians 4:1-16
   Philippians 1:27
   Colossians 1:10

**LINES OF THEOLOGICAL CONNECTION**

1. ANTHROPOLOGY
   Finding your personal ministry
   Fulfilling your personal ministry

2. ECCLESIOLOGY
   The members in the body of Christ
   Each member has a particular function

3. PNEUMATOLOGY
   Spiritual gifts
   The empowerment of the Holy Spirit

4. DISCIPLE-MAKING
   Learn from others

**MINISTRY PRACTICE**
**BLOCK 5 - THEME 8 - LESSON 4 (176 OF 216)**
**QUESTIONS**

1. List the two steps in the simple pattern we can follow to start our personal ministry.

2. List three ways we can take our ministry for a trial run.

3. Name two benefits to taking our ministry on a trial run.

4. List the six steps in the ministry evaluation process.

5. How many times should we work through the evaluation process?

6. How can we know when it is time to end a ministry?

7. If a ministry does not work, does this mean that it was a bad idea?

8. Is failure of a ministry always failure?

# 33. REGENERATION / INDWELLING

## THEME: EMPOWERED BY THE HOLY SPIRIT

BLOCK 5 - THEME 9 - LESSON 1

**LESSON AIM:** Show that the Holy Spirit regenerates and indwells the believer in Christ.

**SCRIPTURE:** (Romans 8:5-11)

*[5] For they that are after the flesh do mind the things of the flesh; but they that are after*
*the Spirit the things of the Spirit. [6] For to be carnally minded is death; but to be*
*spiritually minded is life and peace. [7] Because the carnal mind is enmity against God:*
*for it is not subject to the law of God, neither indeed can be. [8] So then they that are in the*
*flesh cannot please God. [9] But ye are not in the flesh, but in the Spirit, if so be that the*
*Spirit of God dwell in you. Now if any man have not the Spirit of Christ, he is none of his.*
*[10] And if Christ be in you, the body is dead because of sin; but the Spirit is life because*
*of righteousness. [11] But if the Spirit of him that raised up Jesus from the dead dwell in*
*you, he that raised up Christ from the dead shall also quicken your mortal bodies by his*
*Spirit that dwelleth in you.*

The church is the body of Christ in the world today. God works in the world, in one way, through his church. In order to work through the church God himself not only equips his people for service but empowers each one of them to do the work he has assigned them to do. The presence of the Holy Spirit in the life of each believer is the means through which God empowers the church for service.

We can explore the presence of the Holy Spirit in the life of the believer through two realities. First, let's consider the regeneration of the Holy Spirit. In order to appreciate this work of God, it will be good for us to remember that which makes it necessary. When God told Adam in the Garden of Eden to not eat of the tree of the knowledge of good and evil, he also told him that the consequences of doing so would be death. Questioning this statement of God by the influence of the devil, Adam and Eve ate the fruit and brought death upon the entire human race. The immediate aspect of death experienced by man was the death of the spirit. When Adam sinned, God left the spirit of man, making it empty, dark, and dead. This condition persists in every human being born into the world. The only exception was the Lord Jesus Christ when he was born in the flesh. The rest of us come into the world with a dead spirit, an evil sinful nature, and separated from God. This condition of spiritual death is that which makes regeneration by the Spirit a necessary reality.

As we have already mentioned at least two times, regeneration is the work of God, and specifically, the work of God the Holy Spirit. Regeneration is not something that man can do on his own. Man can do things which mimic regeneration but never actually come close to bringing it to pass. For example, we often use the saying that we are going to turn over a new leaf. We know that something is wrong in our life and that we need a change so we intend to do something to try to make ourselves act differently than we have been acting. This new leaf can at best be an outward act, never reaching the core of our being where a change is needed the most. Another example is this. At New Years, we make resolutions which we think will make our life better in the year to come. Again, these are only outward changes. Regeneration is a change wrought on the inside at the level of the spirit and can only be done by God himself.

Regeneration is illustrated in the Bible in two ways. In fact, it is more than illustrated. Regeneration is each of these two things on a spiritual level. First, regeneration is a new birth. You recall how Nicodemus came to Jesus one night and Jesus talked with him about the nature of the change that must take place in the spirit of the human being. Jesus said that we must be born again. Nicodemus asked the obvious question, "How is this possible?" Of course, Jesus was not speaking of another physical birth. He was speaking of a new birth in the spirit of man. To be regenerated by the Holy Spirit is nothing less than a new birth which takes place in man's spirit. Among the results of it is that man is enabled to respond to God in faith unto salvation. Remember also that in man's condition of sin and separation from God, he is free to make choices but only in the realm of sin. The choice to believe on Christ unto salvation is a choice that has to be made in the realm of righteousness and man cannot make these choices on his own without the help of the Holy Ghost. Man must be born again (regenerated) in order to express true saving faith in Christ.

The Bible also says that regeneration is a resurrection from the dead. Because of Adam's sin, we are born in sin. Our spirit, which is the part of us that drives our relationship with God, is dead when we come into the world. What is anything able to do which is dead? If we are to express faith in Christ, God has to raise our spirit from the dead and enable it to have faith in God. This is what the Holy Spirit does in regeneration. The same power that raised Jesus from the dead raises us from the dead in regeneration.

Another thing the Holy Spirit does in this process of raising us from spiritual death is that he indwells us. Indwelling means that the Holy Spirit moves into our spirit and lives there. Indwelling is the presence of God in our spirit. Because of sin, his presence was not there, thus the need to be regenerated. In the regenerated spirit, God indwells and from this location deep within is able to begin to sanctify us so that the way we live on the outside matches the new reality on the inside: if any man be in Christ, he is a new creature, old things are passed away and all things become new. From the position of our regenerated spirit, God who lives in us is now in a position to live through us, enabling us to do all that which he has commanded us to do.

The presence of the Holy Spirit in our spirit is a permanent condition after salvation. When God comes into a dead spirit and raises it to new life, he remains there forever. There is absolutely nothing or no one which can change this condition in the life of a believer. Through regeneration, the relationship between God and man is restored, and the good news is, it can never be undone. The presence of the Holy Spirit within us is our guarantee from God that he is going to bring to a completion the work which he has started in our life through regeneration. This is evidence of the eternal security of our salvation in Christ.

Why is it necessary to try to understand these details of our salvation? For most of us, our experience is that we heard the gospel, realized we were lost, and asked God to save us. While this is true of our experience, the Bible allows us to look behind the scenes and see what God has done on our behalf. We were dead in sins and unable to reach toward God on our own. He regenerated us, making it possible for us to call upon the Lord for salvation. The Bible says that both the grace and the faith to be saved are gifts from God. To know these details shows us what it means to be lost, what a hopeless condition we were in, and how we were unable to change this condition on our own. We needed God to save us and this is exactly what he did. To know these details takes man's salvation out of his own hands and puts it in God's hands where it belongs. It helps us see the grace of God unto salvation and to know as the Bible says that salvation belongs to the Lord.

**REGENERATION / INDWELLING**
**BLOCK 5 - THEME 9 - LESSON 1 (177 OF 216)**
**LESSON OUTLINE**

**I REGENERATION**

- A. An act of God
- B. Two illustrations
  - 1. New birth
  - 2. Resurrection from death

**II INDWELLING**

- A. The presence of the Holy Spirit
- B. The position in the spirit
- C. A permanent condition

**SCRIPTURES TO BROADEN YOUR UNDERSTANDING**

1. Salvation belongs to God
   Jonah 2:9
   Ephesians 2:8-9

2. Scriptures which speak of the new birth
   John 1:10-13
   John 3:1-21
   Romans 12:2
   Ephesians 2:1-10
   Titus 3:5
   1 John 3:9

3. Nothing can separate us from God's love
   Romans 8:33-39

**LINES OF THEOLOGICAL CONNECTION**

1. THE DOCTRINE OF GOD
   Sovereignty
   Foreknowledge
   God's love
   God's mercy

2. SOTERIOLOGY
   Election
   Predestination
   Grace
   Faith
3. CHRISTOLOGY
   Atonement

4. PNEUMATOLOGY
   Regeneration

5. ANTHROPOLOGY
   Responding to the work of God in the heart

**REGENERATION / INDWELLING**
**BLOCK 5 - THEME 9 - LESSON 1 (177 OF 216)**
**QUESTIONS**

1. Why is regeneration necessary?

2. Why is man unable to save himself?

3. Who does the work of regeneration in man's spirit?

4. In what two ways does the Bible speak of regeneration?

5. What is meant by the indwelling of the Holy Spirit?

6. What does it mean to us because the Holy Spirit lives within us?

7. What is the practical result of regeneration?

8. Give some evidence from your own life that you have been regenerated by the Holy Spirit.

# 34. BAPTISM OF THE HOLY SPIRIT

## THEME: EMPOWERED BY THE HOLY SPIRIT

BLOCK 5 - THEME 9 - LESSON 2

**LESSON AIM:** Show that the baptism of the Holy Spirit joins the believer to the body of Christ.

**SCRIPTURE:** (1 Corinthians 12:13)

*For by one Spirit are we all baptized into one body, whether we be Jews or Gentiles, whether we be bond or free; and have been all made to drink into one Spirit.*

The baptism of the Holy Spirit is one of the most important doctrines of the Scriptures for the believer in Christ, and yet it is also one of the most abused and misunderstood teachings as well. The purpose of this lesson is not to present every aspect of false teaching regarding this wonderful doctrine, but rather to present its truth from the Word of God. If we can take hold of the truth, we can identify false teaching when it arises and reject it on the basis of its misalignment with the truth. By the way, this is what we should do with every doctrine of the Scriptures, not only this one.

In the first place, let's think about the baptism of the Holy Spirit with reference to the experience of it. The Bible teaches that all believers in Christ experience the baptism of the Holy Spirit. This is specifically stated in our theme verse for this lesson: *for by one Spirit are we all baptized into one body.* If the Scripture says all of us, how many of us can be left out of this experience and it still be all of us? Of course, the answer is not a one of us. Every believer experiences the baptism of the Holy Spirit. If you are a believer in Christ, you have already been baptized in the Holy Spirit. This is not some kind of mystical experience out there somewhere that you might hope to have one day, or one that is reserved only for certain believers. The baptism of the Holy Spirit is an experience that happens to each and every believer in Christ.

We should also say something with reference to the timing of the baptism of the Holy Spirit. If every believer has the experience, when does it happen? It happens at the instant of the salvation of the believer. There are several works that the Holy Spirit does that each occurs instantaneously at salvation, and this is one of them. We use the word *instantaneously* because from the human perspective it is nearly impossible to put them into a chronological order, or to separate them in time. It seems more that these works all happen simultaneously when the Holy Spirit comes into the spirit of man at regeneration. So then, it is at that instant when the Holy Spirit comes into our spirit that we are baptized in the Holy Spirit.

Another important aspect of the timing of the baptism is that it occurs only one time. It is not an experience that comes and goes, nor one that can be repeated over and over again. In our theme verse, the world *baptized* appears in the aorist tense in the Greek language of the New Testament. The aorist tense signifies a one-time action which happened in the past. Without saying it in the words of the text, the Holy Ghost who inspired the Scriptures wrote in the grammar of the language that the baptism of the Holy Spirit is an experience that happened to the believer at some point in the past and that it can happen only one time. This point can help us to see the need to know something about the languages in which the Scriptures were written. God has concealed many rich treasures in his Word in things like verb tenses, moods, voices, persons, and numbers. Studying the Bible languages to any degree can pay off in many rich rewards.

The baptism of the Holy Spirit has some practical results as well which the believer needs to know. These results are true and applicable whether the believer knows them or not. Since they are true, we should know them in order to enjoy the benefit which they provide. First, the baptism of the Holy Spirit means that the believer has been joined with Christ in his death and resurrection. This is so important because it has to do with the old nature of the believer and with sin. From God's point of view, when Christ died for us, he died as us. The old nature was crucified with Christ on the cross and put to death. Since this is true, we do not have to live as slaves any longer to sin. The reason we sin as believers is that we allow the devil to mimic the resurrection of our spirit by the Holy Spirit by raising, as it were our old, dead, sinful nature from the dead. When we choose to act out of the old nature, we commit dead works which are sin. We are commanded in Scripture to put off the old man and to put on the new man. The new man is after God and is created in righteousness and true holiness. We are to live out of the new nature of God which has been given to us in salvation. The options we have are as follows. If we walk in the flesh, the old man, we will commit the works of the flesh which are sin. But if we walk in the spirit, we will do the works of the spirit which are the works of righteousness. Paul spoke of these options by saying, "*Know ye not, that to whom ye yield yourselves servants to obey, his servants ye are to whom ye obey; whether of sin unto death, or of obedience unto righteousness?*" (Romans 6:16). Practically speaking, the baptism of the Holy Spirit means that we can have victory over sin in our daily life.

Another practical result believers can enjoy is that the baptism of the Holy Spirit joins us with the body of Christ. God has chosen the place in his body, the church, which each believer will occupy and from which place we will do our work for the Lord. The instant we are saved, the Holy Spirit makes us a part of the church. If the Holy Spirit came and went from our life, our connection with the church would fluctuate. But since the baptism of the Holy Spirit is a one-time action, and since the Holy Spirit comes into our spirit to stay and never leave, from that instant forward, we are members of the body of Christ. This makes our connection with the body an unbreakable relationship. This is more evidence of the eternal security of our salvation. It also means that whatever is true of the body of Christ is also true of us as an individual believer. This opens many more Scriptures to us which state various aspects of our relationship to Christ and of the many ways in which we have been blessed of God as a member of his church.

Let us close this lesson with a final note concerning the baptism of the Holy Spirit. Nowhere in the Bible is the believer commanded to be baptized in the Holy Spirit. This fact supports the very points which we have made in this lesson. The baptism of the Holy Spirit comes with the package of God's salvation. No believer is left out of this experience or excluded from its benefits. For a born-again believer to seek the baptism of the Holy Spirit is evidence of the misunderstanding of this doctrine. Since it is a one-time occurrence, and since it happens at the instant of salvation, the believer who seeks it is seeking something which has already happened. The better thing to do is to understand the Bible's teaching on this subject, and to live in the wonderful benefits which it provides: membership in the body of Christ, and the possibility of living each day more freely from the power of sin in our daily life.

**BAPTISM OF THE HOLY SPIRIT**
**BLOCK 5 - THEME 9 - LESSON 2 (178 OF 216)**
**LESSON OUTLINE**

The Baptism of the Holy Spirit

**I WITH REFERENCE TO THE EXPERIENCE OF IT**
A. All believers experience the baptism of the Holy Spirit

**II WITH REFERENCE TO THE TIMING OF IT**
A. It happens at salvation
B. It occurs only one time

**III WITH REFERENCE TO THE RESULTS OF IT**
A. It joins us with Christ in his death and resurrection
B. It joins us to the body of Christ

**SCRIPTURES TO BROADEN YOUR UNDERSTANDING**
1. The baptism of the Holy Spirit
Romans 6:1-10
1 Corinthians 12:13
Ephesians 4:5

**LINES OF THEOLOGICAL CONNECTION**
1. CHRISTOLOGY
The death and resurrection of Jesus Christ

2. PNEUMATOLOGY
The baptism of the Holy Spirit

3. THE DOCTRINE OF SATAN
Father of false doctrines

4. ECCLESIOLOGY
   Membership in the body of Christ
   The church as the bride of Christ

**BAPTISM OF THE HOLY SPIRIT**
**BLOCK 5 - THEME 9 - LESSON 2 (178 OF 216)**
**QUESTIONS**

1. Why do you think Satan works to have believers misunderstand the doctrine of the baptism of the Holy Spirit?

2. When does the baptism of the Holy Spirit happen?

3. Which believers experience the baptism of the Holy Spirit?

4. List two practical result of the baptism of the Holy Spirit.

5. What does it mean to us to be joined to Christ in his death and resurrection?

6. What happens when we choose to live out of the old, dead nature?

7. What happens when we walk in the spirit?

8. Where would you say that you do more walking; in the flesh or in the spirit?

# 35. THE SEAL OF THE HOLY SPIRIT

## THEME: EMPOWERED BY THE HOLY SPIRIT

BLOCK 5 - THEME 9 - LESSON 3

**LESSON AIM:** Share the benefits of the seal of the Holy Spirit.

**SCRIPTURE:** (Ephesians 1:13-14)

*13 In whom ye also trusted, after that ye heard the word of truth, the gospel of your salvation: in whom also after that ye believed, ye were sealed with that holy Spirit of promise, 14 Which is the earnest of our inheritance until the redemption of the purchased possession, unto the praise of his glory.*

The journey of life can be long, difficult, and uncertain. There are times when we seem to lose sight of God. We are not sure where he is or what he is doing. His silence at times adds to the difficulty in knowing what our next step will be or in which direction we should take it. These are the times when we are keenly aware of our humanity. We know for certain at these times that in ourselves we are not capable of so much as breathing unless God is with us to help us. These are also the times when we are the most vulnerable to the attack of the adversary. He plays upon our fears and weaknesses. He interjects thoughts into our minds like: "Where is God now? Has God abandoned me?" These are the times as well when something like the seal of the Holy Spirit means so much to us as believers in Jesus Christ.

The Bible tells us that we are sealed with the Holy Spirit. Notice that the Holy Spirit is the person of the Trinity who does the work of sealing. Each person in the godhead has his own work to do and this is one of the works done by the Holy Spirit. The sealing of the Spirit is one of those simultaneous works the Holy Spirit does in the believer at salvation. This sealing affords several benefits to us which can be drawn upon to establish and encourage us in the faith, but also in the times of uncertainty in our life as previously mentioned.

Seals are used in our everyday lives in many different ways and by many different people. The President may put his seal on an official document indicating the authority behind the message within the document. The police might seal a building as a crime scene, protecting it from public traffic. The electric company might put a seal on the electrical entrance at your home to prevent someone from getting in there and touching the power line. Seals have a function in our everyday life and the seal of the Spirit has important functions as well. Let's name three of them.

First, the seal of the Holy Spirit indicates possession. Contrary to what many Christians may think, the believer in Christ does not belong to himself but rather belongs to Christ. We are not free to do as we please. We are free to do as God would have us to do. This is true since Jesus went to the cross and paid the redemptive price for our salvation. The Bible says, "*What? know ye not that your body is the temple of the Holy Ghost which is in you, which ye have of God, and ye are not your own? For ye are bought with a price: therefore glorify God in your body, and in your spirit, which are God's.*" (1 Corinthians 6:19-20). We belong to God. We are stewards of not only our body but of our entire being. We belong to God from the hair on our head (this is why he keeps a count of them) to who we are at the deepest level of the heart. He purchased us not with corruptible things such as silver and gold, but with his own precious and pure blood. The seal of the Spirit indicates that we are the possession of almighty God.

The seal of the Holy Spirit also indicates preservation. This idea is sometimes stated in other ways such as protection or security. To use the word preservation seems to take the idea further than protection. The idea of preservation is that since Christ has purchased us and since we are his possession, he is going to preserve us from every possible foe which might arise to threaten that relationship. The preservation of the Spirit is another indication of the security of our salvation and of our relationship with God. God is not going to allow anything or anyone to put asunder our relationship with him. The devil is well aware of the dangerous ground he is on when he tampers with one of God's sealed children. He knows we are God's possession and he knows that nothing can separate us from the love of God in Christ Jesus. He also knows that one day he is going to get what is coming to him for the mere tampering with the sealed possession of the Lord in his children. The Spirit's seal means that God is preserving his followers to see that they make it to the very end. He is preserving us from Satan, from sin, and from judgement.

Finally, the seal of the Spirit indicates purpose. Since we have been sealed by the Spirit, we can set out to accomplish the purpose of God for which we have been saved and sent into the world right now. The seal of the Spirit should be one of the confidence boosters we have from which we can attempt to fulfill our general assignment and our specific purpose from God. This is another one of the built-in ways that God has shown us that we can do that which he has given us to do. He has done everything necessary to see that we can be successful. The one thing that can hinder us most from success in the Lord is our own disobedience.

The seal of the Spirit also means that God is preserving us to his final finish line; the salvation of our physical body. The Bible uses three words to speak of salvation and each word refers to the salvation of a different part of man. Justification refers to the salvation of the spirit. Sanctification refers to the salvation of the soul. When the Bible speaks of the future salvation of the physical body it uses the word glorification. This is the aspect of salvation which is in view in the seal of the Spirit. We are sealed until the redemption of the purchased possession. It is the purpose of God to preserve his people through everything on earth until we finally get to heaven to experience the glorification of our physical bodies. Jesus lives today in his glorified body. One day, we will live in ours. The seal of the Spirit preserves us through it all until this finally comes to pass.

Let's make two last comments about the seal of the Spirit. When the Bible says that the seal of the Spirit is the earnest of our inheritance, it is saying that God has put down a deposit, a down-payment if you will, on his total investment into our lives upon this earth. He is saying that what he has started in our life, he is going to complete, and the presence of his Spirit in our life is the evidence to this fact. It is his guarantee to us that what he has started, he is going to finish.

Secondly, this again should give us confidence in God not only that he is going to complete what he began in us, but while we are here, he is never going to give up on that purpose. We have to remember this during the times when we cannot see God, or hear God, or know which step to take next. We have to remember this when the skies above our foxholes are blazing from the bomb-bursts of the enemy's attacks. We have to remember this in our deepest, darkest nights of loneliness and despair when it feels like we are the only person on earth and no one else is aware of or even cares that we exist. No matter what, we are sealed with the Holy Spirit of promise.

The seal of the Holy Spirit says that we are God's possession. It says that we are being preserved by God. And it says that God is going to finish the purpose he began in our life. Now, go in this confidence and be the overcomer that God wants you to be.

**THE SEAL OF THE HOLY SPIRIT**
**BLOCK 5 - THEME 9 - LESSON 3 (179 OF 216)**
**LESSON OUTLINE**

The seal of the Holy Spirit indicates:

**I POSSESSION**
A. Christ paid the redemption price for us
B. We belong to Christ

**II PRESERVATION**
A. From Satan
B. From sin
C. From judgement

**III PURPOSE**
A. Now
B. In the future

**SCRIPTURES TO BROADEN YOUR UNDERSTANDING**

1. The seal of the Holy Spirit
   2 Corinthians 1:22
   Ephesians 1:13-14
   Ephesians 4:30

2. We are purchased by the Lord
   1 Corinthians 6:19-20
   1 Peter 1:18-19

**LINES OF THEOLOGICAL CONNECTION**

1. CHRISTOLOGY
   The work of Christ on the cross

2. PNEUMATOLOGY
   The sealing of the Spirit
   The earnest of our inheritance

3. SPIRITUAL WARFARE
   Satan's attacks
   Using the Word of God to combat the enemy

4. ESCHATOLOGY
   The glorification of the body

**THE SEAL OF THE HOLY SPIRIT**
**BLOCK 5 - THEME 9 - LESSON 3 (179 OF 216)**
**QUESTIONS**

1. Which person of the Trinity seals the believer in Christ?

2. List three results of the sealing of the Spirit.

3. How did we become God's possession?

4. What does it mean that we belong to God?

5. What does the seal of the Spirit preserve us from?

6. How does the seal of the Spirit help us fulfill our purpose?

7. What is the goal of the seal of the Spirit?

8. Share your thoughts on the future glorification of your body.

## 36. THE FILLING OF THE HOLY SPIRIT

## THEME: EMPOWERED BY THE HOLY SPIRIT

BLOCK 5 - THEME 9 - LESSON 4

**LESSON AIM:** Share the benefits of the filling of the Holy Spirit.

**SCRIPTURE:** (Ephesians 5:18-21)

*18 And be not drunk with wine, wherein is excess; but be filled with the Spirit;*
*19 Speaking to yourselves in psalms and hymns and spiritual songs, singing and making melody in your heart to the Lord; 20 Giving thanks always for all things unto God and the Father in the name of our Lord Jesus Christ; 21 Submitting yourselves one to another in the fear of God.*

God has done everything necessary to see that his people can do everything that he wants them to do. He has not left us to ourselves but has given us the divine enablement to live and do as he commands. The primary means through which his enablement comes to us is through the Holy Spirit.

In the lessons of this theme, we have looked at several works of the Holy Spirit in the life of a believer. While the Holy Spirit does many works, there are at least four that he does in our life at the instant of salvation. We have said that these works seem to happen simultaneously when we are saved. At salvation, the Holy Spirit does the work of regeneration. This is the raising of our spirit from spiritual death, also called the new birth. He indwells us, or comes to live within us. He baptizes us, making us a member of the body of Christ. And, he seals us, guaranteeing that what God has started in our life, he is going to bring to completion. These works are one-time works. They cannot be undone therefore they are not repeated in the life of the believer.

There is another work which the Holy Ghost does in the believer, however, which is done many times throughout our life. This is the work of the filling of the Holy Spirit. It is the filling of the Holy Spirit that empowers us for daily life and everything that goes with it. To be filled with the Spirit simply means to be under the influence of the Holy Spirit, or to walk in the Spirit. This is the condition in which we should seek to live every day. The filling of the Spirit helps us face and respond to every aspect of life on a spiritual level.

The filling of the Holy Spirit is an ongoing work by the Spirit in our life. It is the way that God empowers us for his purpose in the world. When we study the way God empowered people in the Bible, we see two situations in which he did this. First, there were times when God had a special assignment for someone and the Spirit of the Lord came upon them, enabling them to do the assignment they had been given. In the Old Testament, the ministry of the Holy Spirit was different than that of the New Testament. In the Old Testament, the Holy Spirit apparently did not abide with the people of God on an ongoing basis. He came upon them to empower them for their assignment and went away after the work was done. In the New Testament and into today, the Holy Spirit indwells the people of God, making it possible to live at all times under the influence of the Holy Spirit. This being possible should encourage us to be more intentional and urgent in the work God has given us to do at this time in history. This, therefore, is the second situation in which God empowered his people. He empowered them for daily living.

From our theme verse, we are commanded to be filled with the Spirit. That is, we should seek to live our life each day, moment by moment, under the influence of the Holy Spirit. Many factors contribute to whether we do this or not. There are some steps we can take which can lead to our walking in the Spirit. We will mention three of them. These steps are not a recipe we can follow like baking a cake, but they are things we can do from a human stand point which will put us into a position for the God who lives within us to live through us, and this, after all, is the point of being Spirit filled.

The first requirement for being filled with the Spirit is salvation. This should go without saying. A person has to be saved to be Spirit filled. God does not fill the lost with his Spirit for daily living. This is a blessing only for those who believe in Jesus Christ unto salvation. If you are saved, you are a candidate for the filling of the Spirit.

Second, if those who are saved want to be filled with the Spirit, they have to surrender to the will of God. God is working all things in the world according to his purpose. If we want our lives to be pleasing to God, we have to align with his will. We have to live and work toward the same purpose for which God is working in the world. This is an area of life in which every Christian faces the constant battle of living for self or living for God. It is a struggle, and one that is ongoing. It only gets easier to deal with when we surrender to God's will and keep our commitment to him.

Next, if those who are saved and surrendered to the will of God want to be filled with the Spirit, they have to undergo the process of spiritual growth. We call this sanctification. It is not the will of the Lord for his people that they never progress in spiritual maturity. In like manner that we grow physically, we are to grow spiritually. Spiritual growth is a process that does not happen by itself; it has to be fed. We feed our spirit from God's Word through reading, studying, understanding, and applying it to our entire life. The more we do this, the more we grow in Christ. The more we grow in Christ, the more likely we are to be filled with the Spirit of God.

Sanctification, as we said is a process. It is positional, that is, it means that God has set us apart for his glory and use. Sanctification is progressive. It is a progression in spiritual growth. And, sanctification is personal. As God does his work of sanctification in our soul, it will bring us to begin to make some personal decisions regarding how we live in this world. Writing to the Ephesians, Paul addressed the idea of personal sanctification in chapter four, verse twenty to chapter five verse twenty one. He talked about the daily decision we must make to put off the old man and to put on the new man. The old man, the old sinful nature, manifests itself through things like lying, anger, giving place to the devil in our life, stealing, profanity, grieving the Holy Spirit, bitterness, wrath, slander, unforgiveness, fornication, covetousness, idolatry and so on. The new man manifests itself in love, forgiveness, honest work, walking in the light of the Lord, producing the fruit of the Spirit, seeking to fulfill the will of God, wisdom, and worship. When these things are coming forth from our life, we can be sure that we are being filled with the Spirit of God and that we are walking in the Spirit.

God's will is that his people walk in the Spirit. We cannot fellowship with darkness and walk in the Spirit at the same time. When we were lost, we walked in spiritual darkness. We were under the influence of the spirit of the devil. Now that we are in Christ, we are to put off the works of darkness and live as children of light. In the same way that God has set us aside for his use, we are to set ourselves aside for God's use. When we submit to God's will, put off the old man, and put on the new man in Christ, the Spirit of God will well up in us as a fountain of living water and he will live through us, empowering us for the work God has given us to do.

**THE FILLING OF THE HOLY SPIRIT**
**BLOCK 5 - THEME 9 - LESSON 4 (180 OF 216)**
**LESSON OUTLINE**

The filling of the Spirit:

**I SIMULTANEOUS WORKS OF THE HOLY SPIRIT AT SALVATION**

- A. Regeneration
- B. Indwelling
- C. Baptizing
- D. Sealing

**II THE ONGOING WORK OF THE HOLY SPIRIT - THE FILLING OF THE SPIRIT**

- A. God's empowerment of his people
  - 1. For special service
  - 2. For daily living
- B. Contributing factors to the filling of the Spirit
  - 1. Salvation
  - 2. Surrender to the will of God
  - 3. Sanctification
    - a. Put off the old man
    - b. Put on the new man

**SCRIPTURES TO BROADEN YOUR UNDERSTANDING**

1. The filling of the Spirit
   John 14-16
   Ephesians 4:20-5:21
   Galatians 5:16-26

**LINES OF THEOLOGICAL CONNECTION**

1. PNEUMATOLOGY
   The works of the Holy Spirit
   The fruit of the Holy Spirit
   The filling of the Holy Spirit

2. THE DOCTRINE OF SATAN
   The works of the flesh

3. SOTERIOLOGY
   Sanctification

4. ANTHROPOLOGY
   Walking in the Spirit

**THE FILLING OF THE HOLY SPIRIT**
**BLOCK 5 - THEME 9 - LESSON 4 (180 OF 216)**
**QUESTIONS**

1. What is God's primary means of enabling the believer to fulfill his mission in the world?

2. List the four simultaneous works of the Holy Spirit in the believer's life at salvation.

3. Why can these works of the Holy Spirit never be repeated?

4. What is regeneration?

5. What does it mean to be indwelt by the Holy Spirit?

6. What is the work of the Holy Spirit which is repeated in the life of a believer?

7. What does the filling of the Spirit do for the believer?

8. What evidence can we have that we are filled with the Spirit of God?

# ANSWERS KEY TO LESSON QUESTIONS

**CHAPTER 1**
**QUESTIONS ANSWER KEY**

1. How do we learn what God has told us about the church and its mission in the world?
   From the Bible

2. What illustration does the Bible use for the church?
   The Bible illustrates the church with the body.

3. In what ways is the church like a body?
   Like a body, the church is one body, made up on many parts. Some parts are seen and some are not seen. All parts have a specific function.

4. What part of the body is Jesus?
   Jesus is the head of the body.

5. To whom does the church belong?
   The church belongs to God.

6. Who has the final say on what he wants the church to do in the world?
   God

7. What are some of the functions Christ does on behalf of the church?
   Christ is the church's redeemer; Christ is the protector and guide; Christ is chief shepherd

8. List five things in the world that stand in opposition to Christ as head of the church.
   Principalities, powers, might, dominion, names

9. What part of the body of Christ do you think you are?
   Students answer.

**CHAPTER 2**
**QUESTIONS ANSWER KEY**

1. Name one thing from this lesson of which a Christian must remind himself.
   That he is a member of the body of Christ

2. What is a great benefit of being a member of the body of Christ?
   In the body of Christ we find significance and belonging

3. What is the purpose of having people in specific positions in the body?
   Christ has given gifts to the church; God has given us a place in the body to function for the encouragement and building up of others in the body

4. Why is it important that a Christian find his place in the body of Christ?
   To fulfill his role in the body and to help the body be healthy

5. What one thing should we consider in all of our decisions?
   The body of Christ and what our actions will do to it

6. By whose standard are we to measure ourself?
   Christ's standards

7. Why is it important to measure yourself by the standard of Christ?
   Because the Bible tells us to, and it helps us to become like Christ

8. Why does reading the Bible anchor us when our faith is shaken?
   The Bible gives us the heart, mind and will of God and will prevent us from being deceived by the adversary

**CHAPTER 3**
**QUESTIONS ANSWER KEY**

1. What percentage of Southern Baptist churches are struggling to continue their ministry?
   80%

2. List three reasons from this lesson why churches may struggle.
   Poor pastoral leadership; power struggles; church refuses to be led

3. What can be the same reason for many different problems in the church and in individual lives?
   Christ is not in first place

4. What is the difference in the meaning of prominence and preeminence?
   Prominence is to be recognized as important but not exclusive; Preeminence is to be in first place in all things <u>and</u> all the time.

5. When we use the expression "the preeminence of Christ" what do we mean?
   We recognize and acknowledge the place Jesus hold in all things....first place

6. Who spoke "I am Alpha and Omega, the beginning and the end, the first and the last" and what is being said to us?
   Jehovah God in OT first spoke it about himself then Jesus spoke it to his disciple indicating that he and the Father are one and the same God and we should give him first place in our lives.

7. In your own life, would you say that Christ has no place at all, that he is prominent, or that he is preeminent?
   Student response

8. What is Christ's purpose for the church and what did he accomplish to fulfill this purpose?
   Christ is on a rescue mission. His purpose is rescuing spiritually dead peoples of the earth by his act of bringing salvation through him by his death on the cross. The Great Commission should be the church's priority.

9. What is the Great Commission?
   The act of going to all people with the message of the good news of salvation through Jesus Christ and making disciples of them

**CHAPTER 4**
**QUESTIONS ANSWER KEY**

1. What relationship mirrors the relationship between a husband and a wife?
   The relationship between Christ and the church

2. In the model relationship between Christ and the church, what part is Christ like and what part is the church?
   Christ is the husband and the church is his bride (wife)

3. What three things does Christ do for the church?
   He gave himself for it; He nourishes it; he cherishes it

4. Where can we go to find the best advice to help in our relationships in this life? How is it helpful?
   The Bible has specific instructions on any relationship we encounter. God's Word is a lamp and a light to give us answers

5. How is marriage like salvation?
   Marriage saves us from things like loneliness and selfishness

6. Why do you think some people think they have to clean up their life before coming to Christ?
   Some may feel they're not good enough to come; others may feel they are the only one who can make changes in their personal lives and do not recognize that they can never do it themselves

7. Whose job is it to clean up the believing sinner? Why?
   Jesus Christ; he is the only worthy one who can cleanse our sin through his blood and work on the cross

8. How do you think we can model Christ's love for the church in our marriage relationships?
   Student response

9. What do you think our relationship with Christ should say about our commitment to our spouse?
   Our relationship with Christ is permanent. We should be committed to our spouse until death.

**CHAPTER 5**
**QUESTIONS ANSWER KEY**

1. What is the difference between the two bodies of Christ?
   One is his physical body - the other is the mystical body called the church

2. List some things Jesus experienced in his physical body.
   Hunger, thirst, fatigue, sorrow, weeping, death, resurrection

3. Jesus experienced life as we experience it. How do you feel about the fact that Jesus knows how you feel when you experience unpleasant things in life?
   Student response

4. Read Matthew chapters 26-28. What other characteristics of humanity can you pick out from this experience in the life of Jesus?
   Student response

5. To be a part of the mystical body of Christ, the church, one must be a believer in Jesus Christ. Are you part of the body of Christ?
   Student response

6. The Bible teaches that Jesus is coming back to the earth and will rule the world for 1,000 years. This is called the Millennial Reign of Christ. Christians will rule and reign with him in this kingdom. Have you given any thought to this future kingdom to come and to your role in it?
   Student response

**CHAPTER 6**
**QUESTIONS ANSWER KEY**

1. What is the theological study of the principles of Bible interpretation called?
   Hermeneutics

2. List Paul's three illustrations of the church.
   Body, building, bride

3. What role do you play in the body of Christ?
   Student response

4. Every role in the body of Christ is important. What benefit does your role provide to the church?
   Student response

5. Two specific ways that we show our respect for the church are by our regular attendance and support. Are you a faithful attender and supporter of the local church?
   Student response

**CHAPTER 7**
**QUESTIONS ANSWER KEY**

1. What is a Gentile?
   Anyone other than a Jew

2. What great truth do we need to grasp as a Christian?
   The church is the context for our life on earth

3. What source of frustration hinders us from living in the context of the church?
   Trying to live a dual life: a selfish life or one committed to God

4. Do you struggle with this frustration? Explain.
   Student response

5. What is indicated when a Christian continually gives in to this frustration?
   That he is not fully committed to God

6. What will it mean for the church to be the context for your life?
   You will make your decisions based on their effect on the church; you will live for something bigger than yourself

7. What does it mean to you that God has selected a specific place in his body just for you?
   Student response

8. List four blessings of having a place in the body of Christ.
   Belonging; contribution; purpose; value

9. What is your place in the body of Christ?
   Student response

**CHAPTER 8**
**QUESTIONS ANSWER KEY**

1. What is our chief aim in life?
   To glorify God

2. From this lesson, list the three conditions for our asking in prayer.
   Ask from purpose, power, and perspective

3. Do you ask God for things outside the scope of these conditions?
   Student response

4. Can you give an example of how God answered prayer when you prayed under these conditions?
   Student response

5. Are you beginning to make any plans to help you make an impact in the world for the glory of God?
   Student response

6. Do you think the way you live your life brings glory to God? In what ways?
   Student response

7. Does anyone in another country know your name? What country?
   Student response

8. Explain how selfishness in our lives can hinder the answer to our prayers.
   Student response

**CHAPTER 9**
**QUESTIONS ANSWER KEY**

1. What people make up the church?
   Those who believe on Christ from Jews and Gentiles

2. List three secrets revealed in the New Testament.
   The blindness of Israel, the church, and the indwelling Christ in the believer

3. Why was Israel blinded?
   For refusing Christ and his purpose

4. What is another word for a mystery?
   A secret

5. Why are the Jews called God's chosen people?
   God chose them to bring the Messiah to the world and to tell his good news of salvation to all people

6. Do you believe on Christ in your heart?
   Student response

7. Do you tell others about Christ and how they can have a relationship with him?
   Student response

**CHAPTER 10**
**QUESTIONS ANSWER KEY**

1. What two major events take place in the book of Acts?
   Israel refuses the kingdom of God; the rise of the church

2. What is another word for a church?
   Assembly

3. What is the two-fold work of the church?
   Evangelization; disciple-making

4. What is the difference between the two works mentioned in the previous question?
   Evangelism - sharing the gospel of Jesus Christ; Disciple-making - teaching those who believe to follow Christ

5. Who was the key leader in the church in its early days?
   Paul

6. God calls people to work for his church. Have you ever considered what God may be calling you to do in and for his church?
   Student response

7. What are the two sending agencies of the Southern Baptist Convention?
   The North American Mission Board (NAMB) and The International Mission Board (IMB)

8. Use the internet to research other mission agencies. Try to see if one of them offers a career that you may be interested in. What is it?
   Student response

**CHAPTER 11**
**QUESTIONS ANSWER KEY**

1. Name the two numbers in which a church should be interested.
   The world's population; the world-wide growth of the church

2. In what mission is every Christian to be engaged?
   Disciple-making

3. List two reasons why a Christian does not multiply.
   Does not know the strategy of multiplication; disobedience

4. On what condition did Jesus promise to be with us today?
   If we obey his command to make disciples

5. What do you think about the growth of the church in other countries today?
   Student response

6. What do you think about the work yet to be done in sharing the gospel and translating the Bible into other languages?
   Student response

7. What are you personally doing to multiply disciples of Christ?
   Student response

8. Research Wycliffe Bible Translators on the internet. Take a look at all the available jobs and careers through this wonderful ministry. Do you see one that appeals to you?
   Student response

**CHAPTER 12**
**QUESTIONS ANSWER KEY**

1. What is persecution?
   Any form of hostility from the world in response to a person's association with Jesus Christ

2. What are some forms persecution may take?
   Discrimination, insults, slavery, isolation, torture, severe punishment, rape, and death

3. How does church persecution in the 20th century compare to that of other centuries?
   More than all combined

4. Have you ever been persecuted for your belief in the Lord Jesus Christ?
   Student response

5. Go to www.opendoorsusa.org and learn about the present day persecution of believers around the world. Is God calling you to work in this area of ministry?
   Student response

**CHAPTER 13**
**QUESTIONS ANSWER KEY**

1. In the beginning of the church, people announced their belief in Christ at the risk of their life. Has being a believer cost you anything today?
   Student response

2. Jesus said we would be his witnesses. The word "witness" comes from the Greek word for a martyr. What do you think this says about the Christian life?
   Student response

3. The early church paid a great price so the church could fulfill her assignment. How are Christians today squandering this investment of the early church?
   Student response

4. What investment are you making in the Lord's church today?
   Student response

5. More Christians were martyred in the 20th century than in all the other centuries combined. We have seen many Christians martyred recently by ISIS. What is your reaction when you see this happening to fellow Christians in other parts of the world?
   Student response

6. The work done by the apostles and the apologists of the early church is invaluable to us today. Thank God for the lives which were given so we could hear the gospel and be saved. Thank God for the writings of these men that help us know God through the Scriptures in our time.
   Student response

**CHAPTER 14**
**QUESTIONS ANSWER KEY**

1. Within 500 years of the death and resurrection of Christ, the true church became overshadowed by the church left to the world by the fall of the Roman Empire. What was an easy clue to know the difference between the two?
   The true church was persecuted and did not use persecution against others

2. The church of the state was eventually divided into two churches which continue today. What are they?
   The Orthodox Church in the East; The Roman Catholic Church in the West

3. In what year did the schism officially take place?
   1054

4. Both the eastern and western churches claimed to be the catholic church. What does catholic mean?
   Universal

5. What were three weapons mentioned in the lesson which were used by the Roman Catholic church to exert its influence and authority in the world?
   Persecution, excommunication, and execution

6. The Roman Catholic Church had much power and influence, was growing wealthy, but was declining spiritually. What term was used in the lesson to describe the church's spiritual condition?
   Spiritually bankrupt

7. What tools do we have today to help us discern the difference between the true church of the Lord Jesus Christ and an imposter?
   The Word of God and the Holy Spirit

**CHAPTER 15**
**QUESTIONS ANSWER KEY**

1. From this lesson, what two events from church history still influence the world in which we live in today?
   The Crusades; The Reformation

2. Who is the most well-known reformer of the reformation?
   Martin Luther

3. What practice of the church tipped the scales for Martin Luther?
   The selling of indulgences (forgiveness of sins)

4. What bold move did Martin Luther make to mark the beginning of the reformation?
   He nailed his Ninety-Five Theses to the door of the church

5. Although it was not the only place where reform had started to take place, where did Martin Luther take his stand against the church?
   Wittenberg, Germany

6. Have you ever felt the need to take a stand for God in the midst of a group which was against him? Explain.
   Student response

7. Do you think you could take a stand for God if it meant losing your life?
   Student response

8. Read Foxes Book of Martyrs about those who died for their faith in Christ.

**CHAPTER 16**
**QUESTIONS ANSWER KEY**

1. What does the phrase mean, "the shrinking of the world"?
   It is a reference to the fact that nearly all people are now within the reach of all others. Another way to say it is, "It's a small world"

2. List some contributing factors to the shrinking of the world.
   Exploration, industrialization, world wars, technology

3. What are the three periods of missionary advance after the reformation?
   Coastal, Inland, People groups

4. What was the controversy in the church during the period of inland missionary advance?
   Whether to do church or to be the church

5. By what was the struggle of the previous question fueled?
   Giving money to others groups to do a church's missionary work for them

6. While churches gave money to others to do mission work for them, what did they do?
   Focused their attention on themselves and failed to prepare for the future

7. What is the focus of missionary work in our day?
   Planting the church among people groups

8. How are you involved in the missionary effort of the church?
   Student response

**CHAPTER 17**
**QUESTIONS ANSWER KEY**

1. Name the two ways that we may think of the church.
   The universal church; the local church

2. List the three questions a local church should ask as it begins its work for God.
   What are we to do? How should we organize ourselves in order to do what we are supposed to do? What are the priorities within our organizational structure?

3. What word from Acts 6:1-7 is our clue to the organizational structure of the local church?
   Deacon

4. As seen in the word "deacon", how does the Bible organize the local church body?
   Pastor, deacons, the remaining people

5. What are the roles of the three groups within the church?
   Pastor and deacons are offices within the church who lead the people to accomplish the church's mission; The people are the work force responsible to perform the mission of the church

6. What is the devil's counterstrategy against the organization and priorities of the church?
   To reverse the order and the roles

7. What can be the results of following the Biblical pattern for church organization?
   The church can accomplish the great commission; the church can grow and mature; People will be drawn to the church

**CHAPTER 18**
**QUESTIONS ANSWER KEY**

1. How many ordinances do we observe in the Christian church?
   Two

2. What are the ordinances we observe in the Christian church?
   Baptism and the Lord's Supper

3. What is the order in which the ordinances are to be observed?
   Baptism first, then the Lord's Supper

4. List some things that are signified by baptism.
   Baptism is an identification, an illustration, by immersion, a total involvement

5. List some things we do as we observe the Lord's Supper.
   We remember Christ life and death, we proclaim his death, we look forward to his return for the church, we fellowship with the body of Christ

6. Why do we observe these two ordinances?
   Jesus commanded us to observer them; the early church observed them

7. Are you a believer in the Lord Jesus Christ? Have you followed him in baptism?
   Student response

**CHAPTER 19**
**QUESTIONS ANSWER KEY**

1. What are the two ways we can think of the church?
   Universal and local

2. What form of government do most Baptist churches have?
   Congregational

3. What is a congregational form of church government?
   The members can participate in decision making

4. What are the two prerequisites of membership in the local church?
   Belief in Christ; Baptism

5. List three purposes for the local church.
   Worship; Discipline; Carry out the great commission

6. Are you a member of a local church? Where?
   Student response

7. What is your level of commitment and participation in the support and ministry of the local church?
   Student response

**CHAPTER 20**
**QUESTIONS ANSWER KEY**

1. What are some affiliations which a local church may have?
   Denominational, national, state, local, other churches, ministers, and ministries

2. What does affiliation with other ministries prevent in the local church?
   Isolation

3. Why is the isolation of a local church so dangerous?
   It can lead to the decline and death of the local church

4. What is the danger of over-affiliation?
   A church may think it's personal obligation is relieved because it has faithfully supported the ministry of another; It can lead to not having the funds to encourage ministry on the local level

**CHAPTER 21**
**QUESTIONS ANSWER KEY**

1. Why is doctrine important?
   It tells us from God's perspective what we should believe; it helps us recognize members of the true church

2. Who should be a student of theology?
   Every Christian

3. Get yourself a basic theology text book in order to study the doctrines of the church.
   Student activity

4. Research the topics mentioned in the theological connections section of this lesson.
   Student activity

**CHAPTER 22**
**QUESTIONS ANSWER KEY**

1. What is religion?
   Man's attempt to satisfy his need to worship

2. Where do false religions come from?
   Satan

3. What is one thing Satan may use to start a new religion?
   Truth

4. What subject is a good test to determine if a religion is true or false?
   What does it say about Jesus Christ

5. How is a non-Christian religion identified?
   It usually worships a god other than Jehovah

6. How are secular religions identified?
   They usually worship man or nature

7. Where did many non-Christian religions originate?
   In the East or the Middle East

8. Do all religious roads lead to the true and living God?
   No

**CHAPTER 23**
**QUESTIONS ANSWER KEY**

1. What are some rivals to the church mentioned in this lesson?
   Non-Christian religions; secular religions, cults, the occult

2. What are the general differences between the groups in the previous question?
   A. Christianity - Worships Jehovah
   B. Non-Christian religions - Worships other gods
   C. Secular religions - Worships man, nature, or no god at all
   D. Cults - May worship Jehovah or not, but with something added
   E. Occult - Worships everything from the earth to Satan

3. What is the general pathway followed by the cults?
   A. Opposes orthodox Christianity
   B. Appeal to the emotionally vulnerable
   C. Take an apocalyptic stance
   D. Promote isolation
   E. Manipulate information and doctrine
   F. Control their members
   G. Make threats to members

4. List some specific areas of cult beliefs and practice.
   God, Scriptures and doctrines, salvation

5. List some known cults.
   A. Eastern Mystic Religions
   B. Christian Science
   C. Scientology
   D. Mormonism
   E. Seventh Day Adventists
   F. Jehovah's Witness
   G. The Unification Church
   H. Wicca.

6. What is our defense from the cults?
   The Scriptures

7. Have you ever encountered a cult member? What was your experience?
   Student response

**CHAPTER 24**
**QUESTIONS ANSWER KEY**

1. What are two general divisions of the occult?
   Soft-core occult; hard-core occult

2. What three things characterize the occult?
   Secret things; beyond the 5 human senses; the supernatural

3. List three ways in which we are exposed to the occult.
   Media; friends; society

4. Give an example of soft-core occult practices.
   Horoscopes

5. Give an example of hard-core occult practices.
   Satanism

6. Where have you noticed the occult in the community?
   Student response

7. Have you ever participated in an occult activity? What was it?
   Student response

8. What should you do if you have any occult items in your possession?
   (Acts 19:18-20)
   Student response

**CHAPTER 25**
**QUESTIONS ANSWER KEY**

1. Where is desire found?
   In the heart

2. What is the heart?
   The true person we are on the inside

3. What can our heart's desire reveal to us?
   God's purpose for our life upon the earth

4. List two ways we can encounter desire.
   Longing; the negative and opposite pull of the enemy

5. How can you begin to discover your hearts true desire?
   By examining your life, asking specific questions

6. Why does the enemy seek to keep your desire concealed from you?
   So you will not fulfill God's purpose for your life

7. Have you begun the search for your heart's desire? Have you discovered it yet? What is it?
   Student response

8. Visit the Billy Graham Library in Charlotte, NC to see the impact one life can make when lived out of the desire of the heart.
   Student activity

**CHAPTER 26**
**QUESTIONS ANSWER KEY**

1. How many categories of spiritual gifts are there in Romans twelve?
   Seven

2. How many gifts does a believer have?
   At least one; maybe more than one

3. Are we relieved of service if we do not have a particular gift that may be needed in a given situation?
   No because the Holy Spirit can empower us to do what is needed

4. Have you discovered which one of the seven gifts in Romans twelve that you have?
   Student response

5. How are you currently using your spiritual gift?
   Student response

6. What kind of ministry could you develop out of your spiritual gift?
   Student response

7. Are you able to recognize the spiritual gifts of other believers? Who and what?
   Student response

8. Are you helping others to discover their spiritual gift?
   Student response

**CHAPTER 27**
**QUESTIONS ANSWER KEY**

1. List the four things with which God has equipped us for the ministry.
   Desire, spiritual gifts, talents, and skills

2. What is the difference between a talent and a skill?
   Talent - an natural ability; Skill - an acquired ability

3. What is your heart's desire?
   Student response

4. What is your spiritual gift?
   Student response

5. What are your talents?
   Student response

6. What are your skills?
   Student response

7. How are you presently using your equipment in the Lord's service?
   Student response

8. What ministry could you do which would incorporate all of your equipment for God?
   Student response

**CHAPTER 28**
**QUESTIONS ANSWER KEY**

1. What is another name for mentoring?
   Disciple-making

2. What is mentoring?
   The process of making a disciple

3. What two mentoring principles do we find in the example of Philip?
   The principle of presence; the principle of guidance

4. What is the principle of presence?
   Investing time into the life of another believer

5. What is the principle of guidance?
   Teaching the believer to grow and reproduce spiritually

6. Who is expected of God to be a disciple-maker, or a mentor?
   Every believer in Christ

7. Have you been mentored to the point of spiritual reproduction? If so, by whom?
   Student response

8. Are you mentoring anyone presently, or have plans to do so in the future?
   Student response

**CHAPTER 29**
**QUESTIONS ANSWER KEY**

1. What is the description of a Godly dream?
   A dream for ministry is more the development of processed information. It is the conclusion we get when we have considered all the factors involved in our life on earth from God's point of view.

2. What can God do with our dreams?
   He can make it more than we ever dreamed of

3. What should our dream for ministry consider?
   What God is doing, where he is working, how we are equipped, our desire

4. What is the one thing we should never do with a dream for ministry?
   Not try it

5. Where does a dream for ministry come from?
   From God

6. Do you have a dream for ministry? What is it?
   Student response

7. Have you tried your dream for ministry?
   Student response

8. What did you learn?
   Student response

**CHAPTER 30**
**QUESTIONS ANSWER KEY**

1. How is the call to ministry connected to salvation?
   God saves that he might send; the call to salvation is the call to serve

2. What is God's general purpose for all of us?
   To make disciples of all nations

3. Have you discovered God's specific purpose for your life?
   Student response

4. Will God ever take back his call on your life to service?
   No

5. Give some examples of standard ministry.
   Evangelism, disciple-making, church attendance, supporting the church financially, and giving a general Christian witness for Christ where ever we go

6. Give some examples of specialized ministry.
   Pastoral service, missionary service, music ministry, student ministry, parachurch ministry, or non-profit Christian ministry, or whatever we may call doing a ministry and making a living from it at the same time

7. How would you grade your performance in standard ministry at the present time?
   Student response

8. Is there a specialized ministry that you are considering doing for God? What is it?
   Student response

**CHAPTER 31**
**QUESTIONS ANSWER KEY**

1. What is the ultimate goal of every ministry?
   To fulfill the Great Commission

2. What should we do as one of the first steps in preparing for ministry?
   Make a plan for our ministry

3. What is an important thing to remember about a plan?
   Plans often need to be adjusted on the fly

4. What two things can contribute to failure in ministry?
   Failing to prepare; failing to adjust a faulty plan

5. What two important things should we learn as we research our ministry?
   Who we will minister to; where we will serve

6. What form of education should all ministers engage in?
   Informal education

7. What form of education is often necessary in order to perform some ministries?
   Formal education

8. Research the Christian colleges and universities in your state. Note the fields of service for which they can prepare you. Does one of them catch your eye?
   Student activity

**CHAPTER 32**
**QUESTIONS ANSWER KEY**

1. List the two steps in the simple pattern we can follow to start our personal ministry.
   Practice, performance

2. List three ways we can take our ministry for a trial run.
   Start on a small scale; work with others; try it on our own

3. Name two benefits to taking our ministry on a trial run.
   It can help us identify and correct early problems; it can expose the enemy

4. List the six steps in the ministry evaluation process.
   Attempt, Assess, Admit, Adjust, Apply, Again

5. How many times should we work through the evaluation process?
   Until we get the results we are looking for

6. How can we know when it is time to end a ministry?
   When it is no longer needed; when God leads otherwise

7. If a ministry does not work, does this mean that it was a bad idea?
   No - Timing or place or both may be the reason for failure

8. Is failure of a ministry always failure?
   No - God can be glorified by our obedience to attempt a work for him

**CHAPTER 33**
**QUESTIONS ANSWER KEY**

1. Why is regeneration necessary?
   Because sin separated us from God

2. Why is man unable to save himself?
   He is dead in trespasses and sins

3. Who does the work of regeneration in man's spirit?
   God, the Holy Spirit

4. In what two ways does the Bible speak of regeneration?
   As a new birth; as a resurrection from the dead

5. What is meant by the indwelling of the Holy Spirit?
   The Holy Spirit lives within us in salvation

6. What does it mean to us because the Holy Spirit lives within us?
   We are eternally secure in our salvation; God is always with us

7. What is the practical result of regeneration?
   We are enabled to call upon Christ for salvation

8. Give some evidence from your own life that you have been regenerated by the Holy Spirit.
   Student response

**CHAPTER 34**
**QUESTIONS ANSWER KEY**

1. Why do you think Satan works to have believers misunderstand the doctrine of the baptism of the Holy Spirit?
   Student response

2. When does the baptism of the Holy Spirit happen?
   At the instant of salvation

3. Which believers experience the baptism of the Holy Spirit?
   All of them

4. List two practical result of the baptism of the Holy Spirit.
   Believers are joined to Christ in his death and resurrection; believers are joined to the body of Christ

5. What does it mean to us to be joined to Christ in his death and resurrection?
   Our sinful nature has been killed and we do not have to live as slaves to sin

6. What happens when we choose to live out of the old, dead nature?
   We walk in the flesh and commit sins

7. What happens when we walk in the spirit?
   We do works of righteousness

8. Where would you say that you do more walking; in the flesh or in the spirit?
   Student response

**CHAPTER 35**
**QUESTIONS ANSWER KEY**

1. Which person of the Trinity seals the believer in Christ?
   The Holy Spirit

2. List three results of the sealing of the Spirit.
   We are God's possession; God is preserving us; God is going to fulfill his purpose in us

3. How did we become God's possession?
   Jesus bought us with his blood

4. What does it mean that we belong to God?
   We are not free to do as we please but free to do his will

5. What does the seal of the Spirit preserve us from?
   Satan, Sin, Judgement

6. How does the seal of the Spirit help us fulfill our purpose?
   It gives us confidence in God that he is with us to empower us for our work

7. What is the goal of the seal of the Spirit?
   To make sure that our bodies experience glorification

8. Share your thoughts on the future glorification of your body.
   Student response

**CHAPTER 36**
**QUESTIONS ANSWER KEY**

1. What is God's primary means of enabling the believer to fulfill his mission in the world?
   The Holy Spirit

2. List the four simultaneous works of the Holy Spirit in the believer's life at salvation.
   Regeneration; Indwelling; Baptism; Sealing

3. Why can these works of the Holy Spirit never be repeated?
   Because they can never be undone

4. What is regeneration?
   The resurrection of man's dead spirit; also called the new birth

5. What does it mean to be indwelt by the Holy Spirit?
   It means that the Holy Spirit lives, dwells, abides within our spirit

6. What is the work of the Holy Spirit which is repeated in the life of a believer?
   The filling of the Spirit

7. What does the filling of the Spirit do for the believer?
   Allows him to walk in the Spirit and not fulfill the lusts of the flesh

8. What evidence can we have that we are filled with the Spirit of God?
   The fruit of the Spirit and other godly actions such as love, forgiveness, etc

## ABOUT THE AUTHOR

Rev. Allen L. Elder is an ordained pastor serving Southern Baptist churches in his home state of South Carolina for over thirty years. His ministry focus is upon personal disciple-making in fulfilment of the Lord's great commission. Allen is a husband and the father of three sons, a United States Air Force Veteran, and has one grand-daughter. He welcomes your response to his writings. Allen can be contacted by email at allenelder@att.net.

Made in the USA
Monee, IL
19 January 2022